RAGE-IN

RAGE-IN

The Trolls and Tribulations of Modern Life

TARA FLYNN

HeadStuff.

MERCIER PRESS

IRISH PUBLISHER - IRISH STORY

MERCIER PRESS
Cork
www.mercierpress.ie

© Tara Flynn and HeadStuff, 2018

ISBN: 978 1 78117 585 9

10 9 8 7 6 5 4 3 2

A CIP record for this title is available from the British Library

Printed and bound in the EU.

CONTENTS

REPEAL THE INEQUALITY

To Mary Flynn (my mum) and Sara Flynn (my sister). Two brilliant and brave Irish women.

And to Carl Austin for his friendship, patience, love and foot rubs.

INTRODUCTION

I am free. For eighteen months, from January 2016, I was a hostage at HeadStuff Towers: two rooms on a top floor in Lombard Street in Dublin where a ragtag bunch of writers, artists, podcasters and what-have-you are forced to make content for headstuff.org. (I was to discover that 'making content' has nothing to do with bowel movements. I apologise to other contributors for earlier misunderstandings.) We were all forced to live in the cupboards or under the desks at HeadStuff Towers, with only HeadStuff-logo mugs and stickers for sustenance. And I wrote for them. I wrote and wrote and wrote for our evil bosses, Alan and Paddy. They whipped us with their words: 'Type that!' they'd say, 'Review this!' and through tears, knuckles cracking and raw, we would. Sure, it was exciting to be part of a site with so many brilliant contributors. Sure, it was stimulating and creative. But the bosses were just so evil.

Anyway, after eighteen months of writing a weekly column called Rage-In, I finally burrowed out of there. I suppose I should have gone down the stairs and out the door, which was not locked, but still, burrow out I did and I don't regret it.

Just kidding! It was great. The whole experience. I loved writing for HeadStuff and the essays I WILLINGLY WROTE over that year and a half are collected here, along with some new bits. And what a year and a half it was. Back when we started, we really could have had no idea what way the world would turn.

Personally, I've had a lot of terrible years. They happen. Years in which bad luck seems to accumulate. Years in which I've been dumped, or broken bones, or found myself unexpectedly pregnant. In 2015 my father died. While I was still in the throes of grief, my dog died too. Although we had the boost of the Marriage Equality vote going the Yes way, 2015 got strange again when I decided to publicly share the story of my travelling to the Netherlands nine years earlier for an abortion. There was some praise, a lot of support and plenty of vitriol too. By the end of that challenging year, I found myself an activist, whether I liked it or not. That's when I wrote 'I Am That Witch', my first piece for HeadStuff. Not long after, I was writing Rage-In for them every week.

And so began a sort of journal of a strange period in global terms. How innocent we were. Brexit hadn't happened yet, Trump's America was still a hilarious punchline and *War for the Planet of the Apes* was a distant metaphor, rather than a possible best-case scenario. What – even as it unfolded – seemed ridiculous, outlandish, an extreme right-wing fantasy that would never actually come to pass, came to pass. And it came to pass while I was writing an ostensibly topical column for HeadStuff.

Now, let me be the first to say that my being a topical commentator is a terrible idea. I regularly turn the news off. I am emotional. I love to get surreal. I don't like to write about things I don't know about, which is a lot. So I wrote about the world's slide into 'The Shitness' through the prism with which I'm best acquainted: humour. Mostly. I have no doubt I contradict myself at times. I don't apologise for that – like the rest of us, I had no idea what was going on. The evil bosses at HeadStuff were never going to squeeze political analysis out of me, so I wrote about what I myself had experienced, or how I imagined things might turn out. I don't think I'm any kind of guru – I'm just trying to process. I'm a crumbling mess, the furthest from self-righteous you can think of, unless I'm standing up for myself or someone else. As you'll see, self-wrongteousness is probably closer to the truth.

I was very grateful for the regular space to write on the campaign to repeal the Eighth Amendment, about which I'm passionate.

There are several essays in this book about that. There are also essays about online life and exchanges: being a mouthy woman means people aren't backwards about coming forwards to tell you how shit you are. I gave rein to my makey-uppy side when I interviewed a saint and imagined a day in the life of Frank, a very real troll. There's plenty I left out: I had plenty of feelings about Beyoncé's *Lemonade*, but I didn't write about it, even though it's all I listened to for a straight month. It wasn't my place.

In lieu of serious topical analysis, I tried to offer pieces you hopefully wouldn't see elsewhere. What I'm saying is: be thankful I edit myself; I held back from spouting my every thought. You're welcome.

As we watched The Shitness take place, I tried my best to be funny about it. But, more and more, I feel that even fake rage is losing its comic appeal. Satire only works with the tension of making anger funny and the funny angry. It's never any more than a kind of thought experiment and thought experiments began to feel like an indulgence, belittling real suffering. The world was on fire. Danger crackled everywhere – particularly for marginalised people. Hatred has somehow become fashionable, fascism has become cool ('Hear them out!'), kindness has become weakness. Women's rights across the globe are being rolled back. Me Too may have happened after Rage-In and it feels positive, but we have to be vigilant: there will be pushback for it. Trans rights are being erased. Gay people are being put in camps. Poverty is rampant.

I found myself – little old self-wrong-teous actor and comedian me – writing about privilege. Or, instead, offering light relief – silliness – wherever possible. Rage was going to have to become action, out in the real world, or it would just burn itself out. Rage, when the world was on fire, seemed like nothing more than extra petrol. It wasn't funny any more.

In this collection you'll find some topical commentary, but you'll also find rainy summers. Religion. Imagined interviews. Mint chocolate. Acting, theatre and the need to pay people for their (our) work. Some of the pieces make me sad, knowing what we know now. One piece is about masturbation, another about boobs. These don't make me sad. Some were written in a just-pre-Brexit London. The rest were written from an Ireland that has a chance to be at the forefront of real, progressive change. Or we can call lies 'balance' and follow everyone else down the chute.

I hope some of these pieces make you laugh. The ones that don't, maybe they at least capture some of the surprise twists of a strange, shared eighteen months. Maybe they give you some ideas for how to laugh at the darkness and still do your darnedest to be kind as The Shitness plays itself out. I think that's the most radical thing we can do.

The pieces have been grouped together according to theme, out of the light-then-shade order in which they were written. Feel free to hop around from section to section. But don't worry; if the going ever gets too tough, we've made sure there'll soon be a silly piece – a kind of intermission – to lighten the load. God knows, it was hard enough getting through those months the first time.

If nothing else, the pieces are short. You wouldn't even get through a bar of your favourite mint chocolate reading one of them. Or maybe that's just me. Sometimes you just have to eat your chocolate and eat it fast.

Yours, spent of rage,

Flynn.

THE SHITNESS

1

SELF-WRONG-TEOUSNESS

DISCLAIMER: Before we properly launch into the book, starting with The Shitness (yep, it's up first; let's get it out of the way), there's something I want to make clear:

I am often wrong, all right?

I'm always happy to admit when I'm wrong. Wait a second. No, not happy. More like: crushed, humiliated, feeling very tiny and never wanting to try anything again or ever even think about leaving the house. But admitting it does make me feel a lot better than standing over something that's wrong, just to maintain some notional rightness.

Rightness. Sounds almost … *sore*. And it often is. It hurts the person who needs to be right a lot more than their being wrong. *Wrong*. So wrong it's right. 'I'm wrong.' Say it. Try it. Taste its bittersweet salty goodness on your tongue. It's probably not as bad as you think.

At school we're taught that being right gets us gold stars, rewards. It gets us approval and that's great. Approval's nice. But it's also fleeting. You will be wrong some other time (NB: I am usually wrong so you might not ever be, but the likelihood is that you will) and when that happens you'll miss the approval. Start to crave it. You'll do anything to get it. And that's a scary place to be.

I get people shouting at me online all the time about how wrong I am. Since – as far as I'm concerned – I'm really only spouting opinions into the void on there, that's fine. I'm often not sure if I'm right, I'm certainly not saying I am. They are only opinions and I'm putting them out there like it's my own backyard. I'm not dragging anyone past that yard, I'm not forcing them to read my neither-good-nor-bad-*just-mine* opinions, I'm not getting a wage from the taxpayer to cover their formation. So I resort to my usual suggestion that these people unfollow, mute or block. Why, oh why would you keep swinging past my page if you think I'm such 'a giant shit'? (Their opinion. And fair play.) That's terrible masochism altogether. I would also advise against plunging an open wound into a sackful of salt, but that's just my opinion. There's a certain kind of commentator, buoyed up by the current Shitness, who calls some of the things I say arrogant or self-righteous. Well, sir, you couldn't be further off the mark. Not only am I a crumbling, unsure mess most of the time, but you could go so far as to coin a term for me: self-*wrong*-teous.

I can't tell you how often I've been wrong. (Can't *and won't*, cos it's much too embarrassing.) Ah, ego; the need to be right can always be related back to it. There's a splash of entitlement in there too, plus the human fact that we all hate feeling very tiny and humiliated. But it's ego and entitlement that lead us down that path in the first place. They stop us from, say, examining privilege. Instead we pretend it doesn't exist because 'we're not bad people and we mean no harm'. But despite our best efforts, we can and do harm others. Everyone makes mistakes. I have no doubt you'll count plenty in this book. I'm just trying to make sense of it all. As you'll see later on, I might have made a few (un)lucky predictions, but actually 'I've got nothing' in terms of solutions.

But back to mistakes. Some of mine have been poor choices. Some have been accidents. Some have been borne of feelings of despair or loneliness. Knocking on a door that's long-since closed because I still have feelings for someone and am overcome with selfish sorrow. Drinking too much when I feel bad and like I'm owed more than that badness. Using racial or other epithets when singing along with the radio, or retelling stories on-stage because it 'wasn't me saying them'. I know better now. I hope. I try. I still fuck up. But I try.

Nobody's perfect, and I'm probably less perfect than most. I get frazzled and cranky. I forget people's names. I take things personally (especially if they're personal). If someone has a personal go at me, I'm not one of those amazing people who can always ignore and fly above it. My tongue's about bitten to its limit. Sometimes I need to have my say, if only to show someone who's insulted me that I've seen them and am now about to forget them. The thing is, I'm not looking to be elected anywhere; only the opinions of my loved ones really count.

Personally, I know I have plenty of work to do. I'm only learning about my own white privilege through the patience of my fella and other kind people of colour. (Let's not even start to list the other bits of privilege I need to examine or we'll be here all day. I have tons.) I realise that some might not be up for this kind of self-examination, not asking themselves the same tough questions. So I try to be kind, because sometimes tough questions are hard to face. It's never easy to say 'I've hurt you, even if I didn't intend it. I'm sorry and I want to make good on it in future.' Or just, 'I'm sorry.' Sometimes that goes a long way.

Just before saying sorry, I once again feel very tiny. My cheeks glow red with the embarrassment of both the memory of my mistake and the anticipation of the humble pie I'm about to eat. But then I eat it. And it turns out to be kind of delicious.

2

PREDICTIONS: WHAT HAPPENS IF THE RAIN KEEPS COMING?

We didn't really see The Shitness coming. It's hard to know how it's going to go. But here's my first prediction:

WE'RE ALL GONNA DIE!

In case, like me, you're easily startled, I can reveal that it *probably* won't happen in the coming year – not for most of us, anyway. Probably. But the fact that we will die someday is hard to avoid in the constant headlong stream of doom, gloom and misery we call news these days. In the past we'd read an article, shake our heads and mutter 'oh dear' before going back to cleaning our cappuccino machines, or whatever it is we did before coffee capsules and ubiquitous baristas were the rage. Now rage is the rage and it's hard not to read yet another paragraph about our powerlessness without going 'Aaaaaaaaaaaaaargh!' and engaging in large amounts of fate contemplation. It's hard to go back to cleaning anything in such an agitated state.

Humans enjoy the distant threat of death – it's the dreadful thrill horror movies and roller coasters are built on. But we hardly need those any more; our adrenaline is permanently at full tilt.

Be honest: when you read something awful, the person you feel sorriest for is you. Your fear is for yourself. For a second, you put yourself in the place of the victims or survivors, but the reason your heart pounds isn't empathy: it's terror. Selfish, selfish terror.

We're all gonna die. That means I am. Maybe soon. And worst of all, our demise is likely to be mundane and undramatic. We've wasted decades fretting about nuclear annihilation when we should probably have been more pissed that our feet were getting wet. (Global warming is real, I don't care who pulls out of what Paris Agreement in a huff, en route to the golf club.)

Which brings us to floods. I can't help envisaging worst-case scenarios: what happens if the rain keeps coming? (This is Ireland, after all.) It's unlikely that Russell Crowe will ever be allowed to play Noah again, so what on soggy Earth would we do? What price survival? Who would you become? Initially you'd try to make room on your makeshift life-raft for your loved ones, but what if the situation were to drag on? Would you hop off if it became a little too snug? Do they deserve your place? How much do you love them, really? Rose didn't hop off the floating door for Jack in *Titanic*, and their love was so big that Celine Dion sang a song about them. Ask yourself: has Celine Dion ever sung a song about your family? No? Then I'd be jealously guarding my own raft space if I were you.

Some people are already quoting biblical texts and saying we've brought this inundation on ourselves *because God*. But I think it's too late for such fun *whys*. Let's be practical. We've made it this far with evolution, so let's harness its power. I've come up with some useful suggestions to help us adapt for where things seem to be headed:

- **(Re)Develop gills.** Obviously, staying above water will still be the optimum environment for a while, but long term (when we run out of floating doors) it's going to be preferable to be capable of staying submerged. Lungs just aren't up to the job. I'm not a scientist, but to speed up gill (re)development I'll be staying underwater whenever I can: in the bath or at the local swimming pool. (Don't have a local swimming pool? Don't worry, you will soon. It's just currently known as 'the park'.)

- **Scales.** Stop moisturising now. There's no point. Try to re-evaluate and cherish dry, scaly skin as an essential evolutionary step forward. Or back, depending on how you look at it.

- **Take up swimming.** Not really evolution, but now might be a good time to learn or brush up on your strokes.

- **Absorption.** We already use this to retain facts – we certainly aren't using applied thought or memory much any more. All we have to do is shift it to the physical. Imagine if we could soak up excess water with our own bodies? We wouldn't need half as many sandbags! Plus, it's a fun way to hydrate; getting those two litres down you every day is a pain. Now you won't even have to think about it.

- **Ditch phoney allergies.** We all know gluten is made up, but even if you've always said prawns bring you out in a rash, this is the year to get down with seafood. Also to being food, cause y'know who your new neighbours are going to be? Sharks. We all have to eat.

And finally, a few fashion predictions for the coming year:

- *Out* – Smooth hair.

- *In* – Permafrizz. I don't like this any more than you do, but there'll be nowhere to plug in the straighteners.

- *Out* – Sandals and flats.

- *In* – Waders. Stilts.

- *Out* – Summer. Winter. Seasons in general. The fashion world has never known when the real seasons actually are, so designers won't know when to start showing asymmetrical sleeves. As usual.

- *In* – Weather descriptions such as 'plummet', 'cascade', 'melt' and 'destroy'.

- *This year's breakout celebs*: meteorologists.

Basically, what I'm saying in terms of the future is, 'I hope it stays fine for us.'

3

2026:
REVIEWING THE REIGN
OF EMPEROR TRUMP

This was written when the prospect still seemed funny, before Brexit and Trump came true.

Ten years into the glorious reign of Emperor Trump – The Trumperor (as you'll recall, he did away with the title of 'president' and the concept of 'voting' shortly after he came to power) – we, his global subjects are still so very happy. Of course we are! We rise at dawn to sing 'Hail to the Trump' at the tops of our voices and upload it straight to TrumpChat for an authenticity check – TrumpChat, as you know, being the app for fingertip Trump news, Trump comments, proof of Trump loyalty and, most importantly, the one-click purchase of Trump products. I love my Trump heart-rate monitor, the TrumpPump. Couldn't live without it. (Might not be allowed to.)

Turns out we were wrong to fear the mythical wall. There was never going to be a wall, because we are all America now, deep down, so there's no need for one. Once Britain left the EU, Oxbridge's strongest rowing teams steered the entire island across the Atlantic. Better to lick America's butt once they realised what a big whoopsie leaving was for a nation so Europe-adjacent; no point having the Eurostar connecting London and Paris once the French turned their backs on their new, non-European neighbours (even though we're all America now). Not only did the French cease trading with Britain at the beginning of The Great Amerification, but they unveiled Super-French, a French so French it's impenetrable to anyone who doesn't live inside France's borders all year long. Now, even the most seasoned traveller can't find out where the *bibliothèque* is. Maybe just as well; libraries no longer exist, so it's a bit pointless to ask for directions to them. But not being able to order a *croque monsieur* or *pression* made the Chunnel trip a futile exercise, and eventually it was bricked up, just before Britain left the area altogether. We missed our nearest neighbours, but as we'd recently watched certain factions dragging them to hell in a handcart, we hoped a change might end up doing them good.

Ireland? Brexit left us stranded in more ways than one. It's harder for the thousands who live in Britain to get home across the Atlantic for Christmas – sorry, *Trump-mas* – unless they have the oars. (Planes were discontinued after the choice became either million-euro flights or Ryanair. People chose never flying again as the best option.)

The Trumperor, of course, decreed that women are just clucking hens and that the loudest cluckers be chucked in coops for too much clucking. This was a huge relief to Ireland's previously silenced Men's Rights Activists (MRA) and politicians, who were able to get on with ignoring lots of other issues instead.

With Britain inaccessible for termination of crisis pregnancies, Ireland was forced back to the old ways – i.e. minimum thirteen children per household – and so the population surged to fifty million. Under the weight of this and other pressures, the country began to sink. Literally. Not the kind of flooding I had earlier predicted, but it was fairly wet all the same. Without the resources other countries have, like oars, or enough money for bailout devices (a TrumpPump is recommended), we are trapped, sinking, leaking, circling the drain. With such a massive population, homelessness is at ninety per cent with the wealthiest ten per cent living in the tallest trees. Those of us in between have gotten really good at swimming (as I thought we might) and this is probably a good time to remind you that Trump products are, of course, completely waterproof.

Irish politicians regretted going public on not wanting to deal with the Trumperor should he be elected (elections? Remember those?) and suffered a televised flogging on his coronation. Luckily for them, sea levels were already rising and underwater flogging, it turns out, doesn't sting too badly!

US population is at an all-time low: gun control was never addressed so the disenfranchised or just plain angry kept shooting and shooting and shooting. As this became a daily occurrence, the Trumperor shrugged and said that this was the way things were and it was saddish ('*Saddish!*'), but suggested that the least painful bullets were Trump-brand ones when teamed with an automatic rifle also called the TrumpPump. There is plenty of room in America now, if only you have the oars to get there and are impervious to bullets. (Trump-brand vests and helmets are fifty per cent off when you buy Trump-brand guns and ammunition.)

There is no news any more, only *NEWS!!!* – a Rupert Murdoch Inc. comedy feature broadcast at 10 p.m. local time around the world. It features all the great things the Trumperor has done that day: opening golden hospitals, turning the sod on mass graves (so long as they're near golf courses), launching genius academies for genius children of wealthy white doctors, and intimate footage of him attending rock concerts and sporting events staged solely for his pleasure – such as releasing journalists he doesn't like into an arena with a bored, ravenous tiger. It's so funny. That'll teach them! Rounds off the day perfectly. What a great, kind man he is not to spit at us through our screens. He could. He owns the technology.

And to think, back in 2016, everyone said this was stupid.

4

THE NEW DECENCY

If you believe the most vocal Brexit campaigners (and many Leave voters did, it seems), Britain restored traditional values the day Brexiteers won the referendum. The vote to leave the EU was a vote for taking back control, for returning things to how they used to be. I have a problem with such reinvention and it's not just happening in Britain.

Ooh, d'you remember when you could leave your bike up against a stone wall and not only would nobody take it, but they'd oil the chain in your absence and leave a loaf of fresh-baked bread and a pat of newly churned butter on the saddle in case you were hungry on your return? Do you? D'you remember? Even the flies would leave the butter untouched. You know, *decent*.

Ooh, d'you remember when you could leave the door unlocked? All that'd have happened by the time you got home would be some tradesman would have let himself in and gone around fixing and tightening this-and-bleeding-that and tidying up after himself and reusing the one tea bag he'd made his cuppa with? You know, *decent*.

D'you remember when a packet of Snax cost 4p? Do you remember p's? Or Snax? You'd get them from a sweetshop run by a woman named Molly or Dolly (like the mixtures) and you'd get a giant paper bag of gobstoppers with your pocket money. Molly/Dolly would always give you a couple of extra ounces to the penny. You know, *decent*.

Ooh, d'you remember when women didn't have sex? Not the good ones anyway (and you wouldn't marry the bad kind). The women you'd know would be good and quiet and able to have a laugh about a bit of oul' touching, or whatever, or else do the right thing, i.e. be wives and vanish? When every pregnancy was perfect and gracefully endured? When (good) women would cross their legs at the ankles only and bake bread (some of which would be left on unattended bikes) for validation. Or maybe they'd blossom into career nuns? You know, *decent*.

Ooh, d'you remember when there were no drugs and no one would have taken them anyway because they were all contented with their lot? *Decent*.

Ooh, d'you remember the three R's? Reading, 'Riting and 'Rithmetic? You didn't need points then, just a willingness to overlook inconveniently constructed acronyms. You'd be straight into an apprenticeship or motherhood from school and it was all good and there was no RUnemployment. *Decent*.

Ooh, d'you remember when the best lad in town was the priest? You'd bob your head when you'd see him and hide your own horrible sinful face and maybe do a cartwheel or two in deference? He could call to your house any time he liked: no need for an appointment for a priest visit. The fine china would be brought out and if you'd no fine china you'd serve the tea and biscuits off the flat of your back as you balanced on all fours, trying not to get scalded in front of a priest. There was no chat of abuse or any of that nonsense and everyone went to confession, so nobody even needed shrinks or whoever it is they all go to now. You know. *Decent*.

Decent. To paraphrase the great Inigo Montoya: 'This word … I do not think it means what you think it means.' Not any more.

This is not just about Britain and Brexit, or Trump's America: we all urgently need to reassess what passes for decency. Traditional values are not very valuable if they don't fit a changing world, or never really existed in the first place. The women and sex thing, for instance: why do we a) pretend it's new (there is nothing your granny doesn't know about sex) and b) suggest that sexiness would make her in any way indecent? It makes her HOT. Hot grannies are just one example of how we have to get real about the past.

Some 'decent, traditional' values are awful. Exclusive, them-and-us, my-way-or-the-highway claptrap. Only in fairytales are there happy endings, and our real-life, rose-coloured versions don't even have giant beanstalks, so why cling to them?

We paint our forebears as straight-talking, hard-dealing, simple folk, but we're making it up. They were as fucked up as we are, doing their best to get things right but often getting them wrong. They set down and followed certain rules that simply don't fit today and acknowledging that does not make us bad. In fact, it's our duty not to remake old mistakes.

'Decent' used to have a narrow definition. It used to look a certain way, dress a certain way, talk a certain talk, go to certain schools, attend a certain church. Obviously, it's still not cool to break into anyone's house – even with the intention of fixing, tightening and tidying. But throwing up into the air old rules and conventions that are only in place because they're 'how things have always been' is no harm at all. I'll bet you some of them are so insubstantial and wispy they won't ever come back down to earth again.

Some people peddle fantasy and peddle it hard. What they're selling sounds nice – if only it were real. That the way things used to be was better. So much better. I'm just not sure that buying what they're selling is the decent thing to do.

5

CONSTANT FEAR AND ENDLESS DREAD

Wait, wait, wait … you're only getting scared *now*? Constant fear and endless dread are *new* to you? Woah. I'm jealous. I've hardly slept a wink since 1983.

It does seem as if the world is coming to a juddery end and that the only thing that might have saved us – given us some spark of fun and unity – was Pokémon Go, and then that didn't last either. Still, I'm amazed at how many people only seem to be getting on the fear train now. I've always been on it and access to twenty-four-hour rolling news has only made it worse.

It began when I was little. I'm sure the privilege of growing up with enough food and little fear of persecution gave me plenty of time for pondering. And so I was afraid of nuclear power. But I was also afraid of fossil fuels running out in the next three years and all the cars grinding to a halt and being left on roads, static beasts decaying and rusting in the rain; of planes (should they still be available) falling out of the sky and of there being no more post. Nuclear power was, apparently, clean, and a good and viable alternative to the vanishing fossils. So my fear presented a dilemma. But I still wore my 'Nuclear Power? NO WAY!' badge like a talisman, as if it would miraculously shield me from the effects of a core meltdown or massive explosion, like Indiana Jones in that fridge.

We were all going to get cancer from Sellafield, as even the fish in the Irish Sea were radioactive. Unlike what sci-fi had led us to expect, however, this didn't mean they could fly or talk or have laser eyes, which was a big let-down.

I had a fascination with disaster movies, so another pressing fear was of volcanoes – of lava, to be more precise, streaming into the house. Though rubbish at geography, I was fairly certain there hadn't been an active volcano in the south Munster region for ages, but that didn't stop me having nightmares about getting the dogs and cats up onto the kitchen table out of the way of the fiery flow. Clearly I knew little about lava, but I was pretty sure a wooden table would do the trick.

In case of overnight fire, kidnap, wolves or bears – overnight anything, really – I had planned an escape route from my bedroom (out the window and onto the lean-to roof below: no need to tie off sheets, the only real necessity was ignoring my massive fear of heights). I mentally rehearsed these manoeuvres daily, even had a couple of actual dry runs. It'd be CRAZY to wait till there was a real emergency to attempt jumping off a lean-to roof for the first time. I also read whatever I could find on freeing oneself from the boot of a car. On any given night, I was coiled, sleepless, under my duvet, ninja-like in readiness.

I was also terrified of:

- Jack the Ripper. The Yorkshire one was bad enough, though I was pretty sure he was in jail. What if the O.R. (Original Ripper) rose from the grave or never really died at all and came to Kinsale to get me? There was so much about him they couldn't explain. Who was to say this wasn't possible?

- Other less-killy ghosts. I'd never seen one, but who could assure me that that cup that fell really was just the wind? It's never the wind, guys! It's never the wind.

- Train crashes, plane crashes, automobile crashes.

- The unexplained.

- The Bermuda Triangle, out to consume the world one light craft at a time.

- Quicksand. (Whatever happened to quicksand? Or being chloroformed, as seemed to happen to Jennifer Hart in every episode of *Hart to Hart*?[1])

- I was terrified that aliens had swapped everyone in the whole world, bar me, for robots and I was being unwittingly nurtured for scientific purposes prior to being mined for something or other.

- Of course I was scared of war. It kept moving around the world but it never went away. The threat of nuclear (aargh!) war triggered by red buttons that idiots could press in a huff or maybe even sit on by accident is with me still. Regular controlled explosions and being frisked on the way in to the airport during the IRA's heyday meant I suspected every left bag, parked car or rubbish bin, so that even inanimate objects got in on the act.

- You could get Alzheimer's from deodorant. Heart attacks from salt. AIDS from sex. Rabies. That's right, even the dog you'd saved from piping hot lava by hoicking him up onto a table could turn on you, were French people ever to succeed in bringing their pups on holiday here.

And, should we survive all that (highly unlikely), we could never

---

1   Consult an elder relative or just ask me when you see me.

escape the ultimate shadow of our inevitable mortality. With years of looming immobility and forgetfulness before that. Erasure. Being useless. Discarded. Unvital. Oh, I'd thought of it all.

So I'm sorry world events have you fretting now, but I was way ahead of you. The world's been ending forever. I've dug a bunker and soon I'll be giving tickets to those of you who piss me off the least, which mainly leaves my dog and cat. Bet they mutiny and eat me within days. And after I've saved them from the lava too.

6

PASTELS ARE WRONG

Intermission –
I know, I know. It's all gotten a bit heavy, hasn't it? I had promised you
some not-so-topical sugar to help the medicine go down. It's relentless
in real life; I couldn't do that to you here. So here's a breather – an
intermission, if you will. Put on the kettle and take a break. Park those
fears and gloom while I deal with something still ABSOLUTELY
VITAL, but a bit less scary.

I'm going to say something controversial here. Pastels are
WRONG. If you like them you are WRONG. Shops that stock
them are WRONG. Designers that work with them are SUPER
WRONG and I'll bet you a million euro that they never wear
them themselves. They meet other fashion moguls and bet and
dare each other to produce lines in lime and peach and bleurgh
which they wouldn't touch with oven-gloves on, regardless of the
colour. Designers, as we all know, wear monochrome, or primary
colours. There is a reason for this. PASTELS ARE WRONG. They
were wrong in the eighties and they're wrong now and everyone
knows it, but for at least six months of the year they are the only
colours clothes come in. Designers and buyers know what they are
doing, and what they are doing is laughing at us, sniggering up
their crimson, asymmetrical sleeves.

   I don't know much about fashion, me in my mostly old clothes,
but there is a universal sartorial truth I've come to learn which I'm
going to share with you. Print it out, laminate it, stick it to your
fridge. Get a (non-pastel) T-shirt made out of it. Say it aloud into

a mirror every day, especially if you will be passing any shops and you have even a tenner in your pocket. You ready? Here it is. Pastel is another word for puke. This is not etymological truth, but it is something you need to learn by heart: pastel is puke. Puke-green, puke-peach, puke-lemon, puke-pale-pale-blue.

Pastels are only half colours, colours that don't commit. 'Hello, blue slept in and will be late for your appointment.' That's pastel. Who wants that? You want a colour that SHOWS UP. A hue that's awake at 5 a.m. to do press-ups, jogs up the stairs to meet you and then carries you down to breakfast roaring, 'I'M BLUE. DEEPEST, DARKEST BLUE.' (I'm not even a blue fan, but I would take navy over I-might-be-orange-who-knows? any day.)

Pastels are polite. But commit? They don't even finish a sentence. Pastels wave you off from the dock, never leaving the country themselves. They ghost you after two dates and pretend not to see you the next time you're both in the same room. Now, I myself don't have many statement clothes. I recently bought comfy trainers online and they are bright orange: the statement they make is 'Visible in crepuscular light' or 'Please don't hit me with your car.' Other than that, the only statement I'm after is 'I'm here.' But pastels don't say that. They dawdle, they hang back. Pastels are never heroes in a scenario: they're the ones who need rescuing. They whine a lot.

Look, I have old history with these bastards. I know what I'm talking about because they've tricked me before. I know you've been there too, so picture this. It's the end of winter. You've been wearing big jumpers, scarves and thick socks. You've forgotten whether you have skin or not and suddenly, even if the actual weather doesn't, the shops start to tempt you with spring. 'Ooh, a cropped leg!' you say. And you start to feel a little thaw in your heart. 'My, a sleeveless dress!' you coo, ignoring the fact that it's displayed near a shedload of cardigans because it has to be for health and safety (anti-hypothermia) reasons. You picture yourself in these items and, while your vision might not be of a beach, it's definitely a warmer and sunnier picture than it's been for months. So you buy the pukey thing.

This reveals another universal truth. Pastels are ALWAYS impulse buys. Why? Because no one in the history of dressing has ever bought a pastel garment after trying it on. When you try it on, the full evil of pastel is unleashed; it has the magical power to drain every single skin tone on this planet of life. From African to Caucasian, no one is immune. Pastels take your own natural colour and make it duller. Greyer. I don't know how this is even possible, but it's a scientific fact. Pastels don't pretend to be anything other than what they are: a range of dyes that aren't quite cooked yet. So why, every year, do we all agree to pretend they're only gorgeous?

No one has ever packed away a pastel for posterity. Houndstooth? Yes. Plaid, yeah, maybe. Blacks, well-preserved whites, royal blues, sure. But there's no point packing away a pastel because no descendant will ever thank you for it. The truth is that you yourself will never wear it again, not after the year in which you first bought it, tricked and seduced by the illusion of summer to come. You might buy a new pastel thing, at the end of another, future winter, when you've allowed yourself to forget the wishy-washy memory. But mostly, nah.

Pastel is puke. It's puke. Give me emerald green, not the mild, sugar-free mouthwash version. Go big or go home, pastels. We're on to you.

7

UNSEASONABLE: DONALD TRUMP AND WASP B*STARDS

Going back to school in September after the holidays was always a bitter affair. If you were from a small town like I was, parents couldn't even sell it with 'You'll see all your friends again!' Sure, you'd spent the whole summer with the friends, eating chips and swimming in the sea. And anyway, there is NO WAY that any reunion would top chips and sea-swimming but at least, back then, you got to do those because summers were hot. Maybe not hot like everywhere that isn't Ireland, but hotter than Ireland the rest of the year. You'd get blue legs from the sea-swimming but it made you hardy.

Once you'd trailed your sandy feet back inside those convent gates in early autumn, you could mark out the rest of the school year with songs and activities. First, there'd be songs about *úlla* (apples) and *sméara dubha* (blackberries), because they were the things falling off the trees and hedges, ripe, into your mouth. You'd have a coat, but you might just carry it or wear it open over your uniform. Then there'd be Halloween songs and masks to make. The coat would definitely be buttoned up by now and you might have added a woolly scarf. Next came Christmas songs and home-made glittery cards. The look that went with this was full gloves-or-mittens and a bobble hat, as well as the coat, now buttoned up to the neck. Later, there'd be lots of holy Easter and Marian (Holy

Mary, not Finucane) hymns and stuff to make up spring. The *bord dúlra* (nature table) was covered in greenery and ferns. There might be tentative coat-opening here, and maybe the rolling down of a knee-sock in the milder breeze. Then suddenly, before you knew it, you were back at the beach! See? There were seasons. You knew where you stood, what to wear. There has always been plenty of rain, but there also used to be sun sometimes. And there was snow. Remember snow? Good. Write it down. You may have to tell your children about it.

I always try to take in both sides of a debate to see if I can learn anything crazy and new, so I tried to stay open to climate change denial. I tried. I stayed open for about two weeks before being put off by the definitive realisation that crazy seemed to be all the deniers had. Even when they try to dress it up as science (and there are some glossy attempts at this), they can't help going off-piste and reaching for their just-out-of-shot tinfoil hats. You know they've had media training to help them resist howling at the end of every sentence like a wolf – a wolf who now moults all year round from the heat and will soon be as smooth as an egg.

Which brings me back to Trump, the emperor of climate change denial. (There's a lot of him in The Shitness section, I'm sorry.)

Basically, as many deniers insist, one isolated frosty day is cited as proof that the earth's seas won't soon be a bubbling soup. Just because you feel a bit chilly doesn't mean we're not hurtling towards disaster.

I'm not a scientist. I'm only supposed to write funny. But even I can see – without long lists of stats or temperature graphs – that things have changed. Are changing. As ever, I have no solution to offer other than laughs. We need to laugh long and hard at all attempts to flout science and take on board what we can see with our own two eyes and feel with our own blistering skins. Then maybe, just maybe, we might have a chance to fix things. I'm listening, scientists! I'm listening. Shower me with your wisdom and preventative measures, for the love of flip! Quick!

It's hot. Maybe not quite 'Africa hot', but mosquitos and flying critters we don't recognise are coming to Ireland for extended visits. Wasps seem immortal now; instead of doing the decent traditional thing (isn't tradition what you all supposedly wanted?) – spending September angrily batting into shut windows before giving up and conveniently dying – they now strut around most of the year, hovering over the Christmas ham, making a din during *Willy Wonka & The Chocolate Factory* and pulling the crackers before everyone's finished eating. They really are bastards.

It seems that, here in Ireland, we won't get hotter summers and milder winters (i.e. a better version of the old seasons, i.e. Spain), but instead one long season known as 'The Soggy'. Warm, moist, windy – a year-long non-season with no variation and none of the benefits of other seasonless places, like awesome polar bear pics, endless sand-dunes perfect for making *Star Wars* tributes, or even something practical like the bonus of great drying. Our tea-towels will be forever moist. No more collages of dried leaves and conkers for the *bord dúlra*. If you can get a GM blackberry at any time of year, then there's nothing new to sing about come autumn. Your cute songs mean nothing, children. Jack Frost will be nipping at nothing and the nature table in schools will soon just be an array of different kinds of wasp bastard.

Let's aim higher and ask for spokespeople with actual facts to hand. Emperor Trump may be happy to let things slide, but then he's probably off having dinner right now with a bunch of horrible wasps.

8

THE MUDDENING

I think it was around the time that 'contrarian' went from being not just a wannabe witty Twitter bio and became a pretty viable job. I think that's when things really went to shit. Now here we are, knee-deep in Shitness. I blame them.

These are never the people out doing the stuff. They sit at laptops and – I can only assume – in large plumpfy armchairs that dust comes off when they hit the armrests emphatically or in anger. The dust particles make them cough, but they still enjoy the effect. It makes them *feel* effective, feel part of something in which they aren't actually partaking. Makes them feel heard. My grandad used to say, 'If you haven't got something nice to say, say nothing.' Not these folks. Oh no. Their whole *raison d'être* is to be seen to be saying. Even when they don't really care about what they're saying. Even when they're doing damage to those who do care, those directly affected by the issue. Even when they have no real clue about what they're talking about.

I'd bet a million euro that they will all have been on debating teams at school. I was too; it can be enjoyable – even illuminating – to take a stance you might not normally take and give it a theoretical once-over. Maybe even see if you can convincingly defend it. That aspect used to make me feel slimy; spouting guff your heart's not in leaves you hollow. By the time I left school for the real world, I had reached the conclusion that entering into any debate should be not about winning, but about what you firmly believe.

But I was surprised to see how many couldn't seem to prise

their fingers off their beloved podium. They simply refused to be dragged from it. Hypothesis alone is the name of their game. I used to take the time to weigh such interruptions up, to respectfully consider this opposing view (like I did with the climate-change-denying wasps in Chapter 7) and see what I could learn from it, but mostly what I learned was how thick I'd been. I'd fallen right into their mud traps, a waste of energy and time. Weighing up this kind of contrary contribution is like stopping to weigh actual mud on an otherwise delightful walk. You have to bring a scales, which barely fits in your backpack. You have to somehow find level ground in rocky and uneven terrain to make sure the reading is accurate. And then, at the end of it all, you realise it was just mud anyway and you could have been breathing in fresh air all along and taking in amazing views.

Indulging only in opinions-for-opinions-sake is bad for your health. A (sometimes lucrative) pastime for these contrarians, it serves only to get everyone else's blood pressure up. It causes you a headache it doesn't cause them. And it's so tedious. You know when you're on that delightful walk I mentioned, with a lovely group of people – it's not always sunny, there's a spit of rain, sometimes it's a bit cold and you don't exactly love every member of the group, but it's still kind of delightful? But then you step into a quagmire and your welly comes off? That's what contrarianism is like. It's like a soggy sock full of the dung of long-gone cows. And then, sockless, you're supposed to weigh and analyse the rest of the quagmire while the group tramps off without you.

Metaphor sludgy enough? Good, because that's what these self-declared intellectual giants remind me of. The aim isn't clarity, or a teasing out of ideas. The aim is a game: Being Johnny Opposite. It's fun for about two minutes in your teens. You might even find yourself dating Johnny Opposite for a bit, till you realise he's all talk and no action. And we need action. Johnny Opposite just stops other people getting things done.

The minute you hear someone calling someone else a 'Social Justice Warrior' (SJW) or similar, you know the ground you're on, and that ground is muddy. People have called me an SJW. Repeatedly. Thank you. What a compliment. I try to raise awareness about things that hurt people I care about and not just pontificate from a dusty plumpfy chair. Thank you. Really. I'm flattered.

But the media loves those who love the podium. They're hungry for those who'll just get up there and spout whatever it is, even mud. In fact, the media are more likely to reward mudmongers (note: mud-slingers are different, these are people who 'mong' it, like fish). So while these are the very last people who will help you get to the bottom of anything nuanced or real, they'll be the people you're likely to hear from most.

There is no doubt our world is going through a period of hardening. Maybe because we're all afraid and find ourselves in permanent defence mode. Shields up. Whatever the root cause of this hardening, kindness is now seen as a flaw. Gentleness reads as insincerity. Sincerity, in turn, is weakness, gullibility. Art must be edgy and dark, or it's perceived to have little worth. Debates must be *for* or *against*, when in real life the truth is in the middle. I just wish they'd stop clogging that middle up with mud. It takes up the space where light could get in.

9

LA, LA, LA, I'M NOT LISTENING

I was wrong! Forget action and challenging the Shitness! Turns out denial is brilliant. Oh, I just love it now. I've been using it a bit recently to get me through and I'm seeing its appeal. It's made it slightly easier to be productive. Made me less fearful of turning on the TV or opening a newspaper. To tell you the truth, it's been helping me to get out of bed in the morning in the first place. Because it really does feel like some very bad shit is about to go down.

More and more, we seem to find ourselves in the second half of *The Sound of Music*, when Captain Von Trapp is suddenly viewed as a dissident for not wanting to display a swastika at his house. By his mates, like! They'd even been in the military together! One minute they were all at the ball, *his* ball, their greatest worry being whether he'd pick the baroness or run off with the governess with the voice of an angel and sass for miles (spoiler: he chooses the governess!); the next minute it's all *Heil* this and *run for your lives* that. With songs.

(I was raised on *The Sound of Music*; my husband hadn't seen it till a year ago. When Ralph, hot young fascist-about-town, comes to call for Liesl, my husband ad-libbed new lines for the captain: 'Ralph, I wouldn't have Nazis in my house and I certainly won't have them in my daughter.' So glad I married him.)

It didn't even matter that the captain had the buffers of social standing, power and wealth; once the forces of evil were in motion, they became unstoppable. There was nothing for the Von Trapps to do but escape, using a talent competition for cover. Sadly, it didn't end so well for the less musical families. But as they trekked up the mountains to freedom, the Von Trapps must have looked back at the balls they'd given and wished they'd been stingier with the canapés. There must have been a few people they wished had choked on their quails' eggs. But at least they had the singing. They would always have the singing.

Do you see, there, how I've managed to avoid parallels with what's happening in the world right now? They're there, we all see them, but it's for my own good. I can't cope with the powerless, empty feeling that the bad shit is coming – again – and is becoming unstoppable. So sometimes I pretend it's not happening. Because it's unbearable. The cruelty and offhand dismissal of others is on a scale I've not witnessed before (and I've been around a while, now). The 'I'm all right, Jack' entitlement to excuse all manner of hatred.

So I choose, temporarily, to dwell on other important things. Like what will I wear to a fancy awards do? I'm rarely invited to fancy awards dos, so to be asked to *Irish Tatler's Women of the Year Awards* is both a treat and a terror – if I get my nails done on Friday, will they make it to Saturday night? If I do my own hair, will I look like a hedge next to the gorgeously coiffed great and good? Will I trip and spill something, ruining someone else's beautiful photograph?

It's so much nicer – sometimes – to worry about these sorts of things.

Like where do you get a vegetable brush? Our last one was a nailbrush from a pound shop but the bristles have recently gone kind of orange. (It sees a lot of carrot action.) We definitely don't want to spend fifty euro on something only a chef might use, but vegetable brushes don't seem to be something most supermarkets readily carry in the non-food aisle any more. Or am I just missing them?

It's so much easier to worry about this.

Like will anybody like the new things I'm working on? Will I ever work again? Stressful, but still a more manageable worry.

Are the wrinkles around my eyes the first thing people see? Before the eyes? Still better.

Is this expensive salad worth it? And do I care about the packaging seeing as we're all about to be blown sky high, or submerged in floodwaters, anyway? What good is recycling if we might not be around next Christmas? Or if we are, what will it look like?

And boom. It's back, regardless. That constant sense of foreboding follows me more these days than ever. I do my very level best to put it to the back of my mind, but at the back, as you know, is where the worst stuff has always lurked.

It's not my rage that concerns me some weeks; it's theirs. And I have no idea what to do about it, so let me put it this way: I'm practising real hard for the *X Factor* right now.

'So long. Farewell. Auf Wiedersehen. Goodnight …'

10

SPEAK NOW, OR FOREVER HOLD YOUR (LACK OF) PEACE

Aaaand I'm back. No longer in denial mode. Well, it seems recent global events have brought about the hard reset people thought we needed. We weren't in control of it (we were never going to be) and it will likely get nastier than we could have imagined, but there's no going back now. Maybe change is good. Though it doesn't feel like it just yet.

Rattling people out of complacency is good. Many who didn't believe that race and gender played a part in, well, *everything that's happened*, have finally witnessed prejudice playing out in the most dramatic way.

Apparently, this is the pattern, how it's always gone: people are alienated from those in power. They feel unheard. They are angry. They are encouraged to focus their anger on other people, different people, instead of the individuals or systems oppressing them all. There is chaos. We reset. Repeat.

At this point you've probably read a thousand essays on that, and heard a bazillion commentators comparing history with what's been unfolding globally. It fits the pattern pretty neatly. Not so neat if you're living it. Not so neat if you're one of the people damaged by one of the most openly racist, misogynist US administrations in living memory, with repercussions reaching far outside their borders. These are mainstream ideas now. They're to be 'heard out'. There are 'good people on every side', is something I hoped never to hear a US president say about Nazis, people Captain Von

Trapp wouldn't even have in his house, but here we are.

Despite the comfort I found in temporary denial – call it res-pite – the attitude that 'it's all over there, just don't think about it' won't keep any one of us safe from the fall-out. The mainstreaming of hatred makes the world worse for us all.

In the past there were slogans. They weren't as devastating as nuclear weapons and with hindsight some seem naïve, but they may have helped delay this new and dangerous reset point till now. 'Make love, not war' said the hippies, dropping out of society in protest, having lots of sex and smoking lots of weed. I'm not going to lie: this sounds awesome. I'd be afraid I'd take this kind of pro-test too far by insisting on using my dropping-out to drink tea and watch *Judge Judy*. You know, *for peace*. But cutesie as it may seem now, young people sticking flowers into gun-barrels when there was a draft in place is a truly subversive act. I'm not sure a young black man would have gotten away with it, mind you, not with his life. Definitely not today.

The Civil Rights Movement in the US had 'Power to the Peo-ple' and 'We Shall Overcome'. Simple. Rousing. Constant. People of colour have had to continue fighting for freedom long after the speeches and actions of Martin Luther King or Rosa Parks. If you don't think the practically routine incarceration – even shooting – of young black men is a real problem, I humbly suggest you do a little research. You can even start on Netflix without leaving your couch. You may be tempted to ditch the research for *Crazy Ex-Girlfriend*, but please do have a look at what people fought so hard for – and are still fighting for – first.

'Keep Your Rosaries Off Our Ovaries' is an old chant for reproductive rights that we still need here in Ireland. One ideo-logy, one organised religion has not only dominated its own realm – churches – but still permeates our Dáil, schools, public halls and hospitals. Though many in the clergy may have been well-intentioned and of course some good was done, the blind eye turned to paedophilia is a massive stain on our recent history. The Catholic Church's regressive attitude to women and sexuality continues to be an oppressive and destructive force, even somehow creeping into our constitution. Scratch that, it didn't creep; it was proudly fought for in a show of might, a symbol of an organisation's ongoing power. Now that the organisation is in rapid decline, we can point to how it renders some of our constitution unfit. This oppression affects lives, even ends them. So, please do keep your rosaries off my ovaries. I'm happy with my current method of contraception. Besides, they sell nice bead pouches. You don't need me for storage.

Many Americans have taken to the streets since Trump's rise to power, in protest at someone who used his platform to promote oppression with hollow slogans of his own. Many of these same people, sadly, protested at the time of the election by not going to the polls, saying neither candidate was fit. I see their point – they were two pretty conservative options – but this is an academic stance. Those theorising or who refrained from voting 'to make a point' will not be the ones worst affected by any new legislation or the already pronounced shift towards the acceptability of hate speech and acts.

'Think globally, act locally.' There's another one. How does this affect us here? We know we have bog-standard racism, classism and bucketloads of sexism in Ireland, but we don't have fascism. Not yet. We have a unique chance to get ahead of the spread of some really toxic hatred. Those drawn to the toxicity are already bolder, but they don't have a grip yet. Call me an SJW. As I say, thank you. Call me a snowflake. I COULDN'T GIVE A FLYING, SITTING, SQUATTING FUCK.

Sorry. But I needed that. We are all in this together, whether we like it or not. It's only together that we'll make it out the other side. The horrible fact is that if we don't stand together, some will not make it out of The Shitness at all.

11

STANDING UP, NOT STANDING BY

People want to be in the popular gang. The ones with the power. We all do. But what will we overlook to achieve it?

Not rocking the boat? Is that enough?

Sometimes the right thing to do is to stand up for others who are suffering, even if you are not personally affected. Perhaps it's even more right if you're not. But something is happening. A twisting. A justifying. Standing up for others is now deemed by The Muddening lads to be part of the new enemy: the 'liberal elite'. Not just part of the problem, but the problem itself. Hate, as we've seen, has become a mainstream topic for debate.

All this has seen rifts growing between friends. Otherwise kind, reasonable people are drawing invisible battle lines, even when they don't realise it. Lines that, once crossed, can't be gone back over. It's breaking my heart.

I was on a train about a year ago. I can't quite remember where I was headed. It was a Sunday but the carriage was still pretty full. A woman in a hijab, heavily pregnant and with two small kids got on. There was a man in her seat. I heard her explain this to him. He refused to move. Politely, thinking he had misunderstood, she took out her booking printout and showed it to him. It was her seat. There was no doubt. From zero to sixty he began racially abusing her and the kids, roaring obscenities, standing up and squaring off to her. Not some young fella, either: late fifties, well trimmed beard, tweedy jacket, country accent.

The whole carriage froze in shock. The woman, rattled, moved off down the aisle. Some other people moved so she could get a seat with her kids. Tweedy (that's his name now) wasn't done, though. Not done with taking someone else's pre-booked seat and being an asshole on top of it. No, Tweedy came barrelling down to where the family now sat, spitting with rage. Actual flecks of hot spittle flew off him. He towered over the lady in her seat. Nobody knew what to do – he was really aggressive. We were afraid. There was no guard on the train, just the woman with the sandwich trolley. I wanted to intervene but was frightened he'd hit me; he certainly looked like he might be about to hit her.

Eventually, a young black man stood up – he was over six foot, so physically able for Tweedy – and gently said, 'Leave her alone.'

Tweedy then rounded on him, undeterred by his height, probably encouraged by the younger man's lack of aggression. In the tirade that ensued, the least offensive thing Tweedy said was 'Where are you from?' Now something snapped in me. My own physical safety was suddenly unimportant. I couldn't listen any more. I couldn't stand by. Shaking, I stood up and said, 'It doesn't matter where he's from. Leave them alone.' I didn't want to, but no one else seemed able. I don't blame them. It's terrifying. We all want to be safe. 'Are you Irish, are you?' more spittle, this time landing on me. 'It doesn't matter where I'm from. Stop. Just stop.' I was shaking. Deeply uncomfortable. But once I'd intervened, other (white) people stood up too. Now Tweedy clearly felt less bold; his shoulders slumped, his volume dropped. He went back to his seat, which was really her seat. I went and found the trolley woman and she agreed that this merited involving the driver. He stopped the train, came down and spoke to a few people, gathering details.

The guards were waiting at the next station. Not much they could do, it turns out – he scuttled off and besides, we have no hate crime legislation in Ireland. But the woman felt safer. Supported.

She was crying, but now we could at least buy her tea and make sure her kids were okay.

At a certain point, it is not enough to be a bystander. At a certain point, you have to stand up. Then you might find others standing up too. Even if some people try to tell you that makes you a bigot, silencing someone's free (racist) speech, impeding them raining their hot spittle flecks down on a stranger whenever they goddamn like. But it's up to us: we can decide not to believe this dangerous spin on the true meanings of bigotry and hate.

The world has reached a place where tolerance of both systemic and overt racism seems to have been fully legitimised. But let's be clear: a business doesn't have to be seen to support discriminatory policies. Customers have a right to ask if a business supports them and have that inform their decision not to use that business in future. I don't know about you, but non-tolerance of discrimination is the bare minimum I look for when booking a ticket or buying a drink. I was heartened that the train lads were on that family's side.

If white supremacist views are readily given an airing – or a Muddening – or seen as legitimate policy here in Ireland, then we are much further down a very dark road than we realise. We already turn a blind eye to direct provision – the institutionalising system into which asylum seekers are systematically put in this country, supposedly temporarily: the reality is more long term.

But the rest of the world has now turned a corner. Looking away isn't enough. It may be particularly difficult when shining a light on hate is painted, clumsily and inaccurately, as the new bigotry. It's worrying. But we can't let it be paralysing.

The world has gone to shit. We don't have to.

12

WIMBLEDONE

Intermission –
Phew, it's a lot, isn't it, the Shitness? Time for a break. How about an
autobiographical story about love of the heartbreak and tennis kind?

I've never been to Wimbledon and at this stage, I'm okay with it.
It's sort of like that moment in my thirties where I realised that I
was not only okay with not having kids, but I actively didn't want
them. Tennis used to be a big part of my life, but it has never been
kind to me, so Wimbledon and I are finished. Wimbledone, you
might say.

We used to go 'up the courts' at school every lunchtime. They
were those multi-use courts that had a basketball basket either end
and in summer you could stick up a net and use the lines for tennis. I think we used them for soccer too, but as I only ever went to
soccer practice twice, I can't really remember. I always preferred the
idea of hitting the ball with something other than myself. Tennis
fitted the bill. And although I'm not sporty (outdoorsy, yes; sporty,
nah) I got good at it. There were pock marks on the gable wall of
the house from me bashing away for hours on end. That wall and I
sure had some times. She was a worthy opponent: she never missed
and she never tried to put me off by giving me the evil eye when
she served. She didn't serve, to be honest with you, but I was always
glad of her reliably sending 'em back.

In my late teens, the best thing in the world happened in Kinsale. It had always been great if you were a swimmer, so everyone
swam: you could go to the beach or to Acton's Hotel pool (out-

doors at the time – we didn't have health clubs back then, you simply either moved or didn't move). The brilliant thing that happened was that a tennis club opened. We could take all the grudges we'd started in school and settle them EVEN ON WEEKENDS. I fought up at that net, and fought hard, and it was at that net that I found out who I really am. Tennis taught me that I am not a winner. I could battle, I could come close, but ultimately I would come second, at best. I was asked to leave the dance floor whenever 'We Are the Champions' came on. The song was not for the likes of me. I still don't like it. But I didn't turn my back on the tennis.

I got a hi-tech, modern racquet for my seventeenth birthday. I still have it, though you could probably class it as vintage now. I've never replaced it. How could I? I might not be a winner but that racquet triumphed over adversity all by itself. My mother's car went on fire one night. (These things happened in the eighties.) The fire brigade came; high drama. They put the blaze out and no one was hurt but the glass in the windscreen and windows all cracked and the front tyres melted from the intense heat. My racquet was on the back window shelf. When the fire was finally out, there was smoke damage on the cover, but the strings, handle, everything else was perfect. I will never part with it, even if I never pick it up again.

I grew up four miles outside Kinsale, in the country. We had a big garden and some fields. The previous owner had tried to make a grass tennis court out of one of them, but it'd break your heart. My sister and I did try to play on it but it was really just a field at the bottom of a hill, beside a river. A puddle, in other words. They'd have been better off trying to make a swimming pool out of it. 'Splop!' went the balls as they landed, never a sound you want a ball to make. So back to the reliable wall I'd go.

When I finished college, before moving to Dublin, I worked various jobs. My favourite was chambermaiding at a guest house in Kinsale town. I'd cycle in, racquet strapped to me, work from 6.30 a.m. serving breakfasts to Americans, then stripping beds and cleaning toilets till about midday. After that, I was free. I'd cycle up to the club, see who was hanging around, play till dusk and cycle the four miles home again. I still came second in tournaments, second at best. But I still hung in there with tennis.

I thought it was brilliant when, later in life, I met someone who was as nuts about tennis as me. We didn't ever get to play – there wasn't an affordable club near us and we were always travelling for work; I don't think I could have got my smoke-damaged racquet through security. But we talked about tennis a lot. We watched it A LOT. Maybe we should have talked about other things, because this was the last thing we did together: we lay in a crappy hotel room in July, watching the greats duke it out on Centre Court. After that, we had to be in separate countries for a bit and next thing I knew, I got a call. Dumped over the phone. 'Splop' went my heart, like a ball on a soggy field that's not meant for balls at all. Since then, the *blaps* and *pops* and scores called by an umpire put me in mind only of a broken heart.

So next Wimbledon fortnight, enjoy yizzer 'new balls' and 'deuces' and strawberries and cream. I really hope you do. But I'll be going for a walk.

13

GIVING A SHIT

It's only recently, as you've seen, that I've begun to wear my SJW status with pride. I've spent a lot of the past couple of years defensively saying I'm not 'nice', not an 'SJW'. I guess I wanted the cool kids to like me. No one wants to be a phoney: it's important to check any phoniness in yourself. But I also probably wanted them to think I was edgy, like them. Y'know, the cool ones. Popular people. But I see it all so clearly now. I had it backwards: they're not edgy or cool. In reality they are – as Donald Trump might say – sad.

Actually sad. Not happy. Perceiving attack and affront where there is none. Inventing enemies for themselves. Muddening. Unable to recognise sincerity or understand allyship or solidarity.

Sad.

But they're loud (boy, are they loud) and they're persistent and tricking us. They're trying to make Not Giving a Shit the new Giving a Shit and it's in danger of working.

A while back I decided I wasn't having it any more. You can have it, if you want. But I want to take back the language they've twisted into word-pretzels and straighten them out. This will make for worse pretzels, but hopefully better words.

Anyone who uses 'SJW' pejoratively at a moment in history where rights are being denied or under threat of being rolled back is a) out of touch with world events and should probably get out of their bubble more and/or b) really, really smug about how their own lovely rights won't be touched at all, ever, and fuck everyone else. If someone calls you an SJW, why don't you say, 'Wait, you're an SJB (Social Justice Blocker)? Ugh.' Make a stink face, while you're at it. Because what they stand for stinks.

So let's straighten out some of that language:

Virtue signalling

Meant as an insult. Fuck this noise. Frankly, not seeing enough goodness or kindness is depressing the hell out of me. Signal your virtues more. Sing 'em. Make a TV movie about them and Roma Downey can be in it and yer woman Laura Ingalls and DO NOT BE ASHAMED OF BEING KIND.

Everything has two sides

It doesn't. Some ideas are inherently terrible and so-called 'civil debate' won't change that. Particularly 'here comes a diatribe about how some discrimination is actually okay' *dressed up* as civil debate. Not everything needs teasing out. Fire burns: we don't have to analyse the truth of it with the guy with blisters on his hands. If anything, we need to tune Blisters Guy out sooner, before more people get hurt.

Until this year I had thought we'd all agreed that universal human rights were where the bad-ideas buck stopped. That they were, y'know, 'a good thing'. Apparently not. But if someone takes a hard pass on your terrible idea, they're not 'shutting down debate'. The world isn't your college society. Other people's function isn't as some kind of sounding board or jukebox for you. Maybe they're tired. Maybe they don't want to add to the raging, howling fury by telling you to your face that your terrible idea is terrible, because they realise you're a person and sometimes the kindest thing to say in the face of an unresolvable argument is 'Let's leave it there.' You know, not contributing to the Shitness. Telly debates have fucked us all in this regard, with their false equivalence and lies-as-balance. I don't think we can change that anytime soon, but we can choose not to take part in this detached debate about what rights others might or might not deserve. We can, at least, switch off.

That doesn't mean leaving bad ideas people to it, or not fighting as hard as them. It means choosing not to be bullet-riddled all day long, or to riddle an individual in turn. It means choosing your battles because you see what's happening all around us, and it looks set to continue for a bit and you're going to need your energy.

Calling out bad behaviour is abuse

It's not. Oh, it's not. Standing up to (and for) people is one of the things we'll need that energy for. If we say 'Mansplaining' or 'Whitesplaining', 'That's racist/ homophobic/rude' or 'Please back off' it's not because we're intolerant; it's because Blisters Guy is back, whispering civilly about how we just haven't thought things through but he's here to illuminate. We have thought it through. We're reading and thinking about how fire burns, just like you are. You're the only one putting your fingers in it. Please don't patronise us. Thanks.

Snowflake

Meant to describe someone too sensitive about things people say, usually said by someone having a hissy fit – to the point of melting – about what someone has said.

Unicorn chaser

Have you tried to ease your pain at the seeming futility of it all by focusing on something not-dreadful? You're a dick, apparently. But listen, dicks can be beautiful things. Sharing good news or cat videos has become subversive. Don't share one today, share two.

Pollyanna
Someone who is vainly attempting to see good through the shitstorm. Supposedly deeply uncool. But have you tried seeing the good in things lately? It's practically impossible. Pollyanna is a freaking resistance ninja. Keep making like her till she's cool again.

Allowing bigots to find other bigots and paint other humans as some kind of wriggling mass is the worst thing global communication has done, for all its connection potential. We've reduced the experiences of others to click-bait terms and debatable theories. So I'm trying hard to reconnect on an individual level. To stay positive. To smile at strangers. Thank the bus driver. Chat to someone in a sleeping bag on the street. Virtue signalling? Too right. Bite me. Let me put it to music for you. TV movie to follow.

14

THE JOKE'S ON US

I think it was near the end of 2016 when I decided I didn't love satire any more. Not in that sort of 'satire is dead', sweeping way so beloved of some columnists during these volatile times. Satire itself, in general, isn't dead at all – the beauty of it is in its ability to pop up in different forms, adapting to the kind of laugh people need at a given moment in history. It might be a jester doing pratfalls with a crown on. It might be the effigy of a dictator taking a pie to the face. It might be a wry poem in a letter to a broadsheet. A YouTube takedown. Satire will be fine. The problem, as I see it, is that we've squeezed it into one mould and that mould is broken. How we laugh might be what needs to change.

The news isn't funny these days. At all. It's chilling. To simply point out or mock what's happening smacks of spite; laughter from this risk-free, luxury position rings hollow.

There can be a safe distance to political satire that isn't always helpful; it's supposed to be the establishment, the man, that's being challenged. So what happens when those doing the satire are steeped in unquestioned privilege? When they have nothing to lose? Not that political classes don't need deflating, or metaphorical kicks to the balls, regardless of who's delivering them. It's the delivery method – powerful blokes in suits mocking powerful blokes in suits and then hanging out with them – that I don't find that funny any more.

During the alternative comedy scene of the eighties, this kind of punch to the establishment was essential, radical, new. But, like the period jokes some women were doing then for the first time, that particular kind of joke, that kind of punching got done. Now this genre of knowing potshot feels almost anachronistic. Tearing down is oh so easy when things are already crumbling. Have we – now, bear with me – have we thought about using comedy to build?

Instead of rallying, old-school political satire can make us *feel* switched on, engaged, possibly at the cost of actually taking meaningful action. Did laughing at Trump and Farage help get them in? Personally, I think that's a massive stretch (and one which diminishes the systemic racism and sexism that were bubbling away all the while). But dealing with them in this particular, be-suited way at this particular time might just have helped us to look sideways when we should have been looking head on.

There's an over-reliance in Ireland on on-the-nose, topical comedy. There were a few years at Dublin Comedy Improv when, although people in the audience were allowed to suggest literally any scenario in the world, they would, without fail, shout 'Brown envelopes!' or 'Property developers!' or 'Do Bertie!' It's not that these things shouldn't be tackled comedically, it's that *they already have been*. And I'm no longer certain where playing things out as they've already happened really gets us.

Our lives, minute by minute, are overflowing with politics. I don't want to hear any more about it. I want to switch off. I know other comics who do too. There are lots of other ways to get laughs; lighter or more surreal material doesn't necessarily mean a pertinent comment isn't being made. Right now, I see these as being of greater service. We need an intermission. We need a break.

Satire can be silly, light, ridiculous. It should stimulate. Refresh. Re-energise. It doesn't have to get caught in the rut of the week that was – it can innovate. More songs, bigger metaphors, tons more craic. When even the most ridiculous politicians have real darkness in their policies, when the world is shifting fast beneath our feet, satire needs to shift too. We need to look forward; what's behind is already in ashes. Mocking isn't enough. We need sometimes to lift.

As the world gets swept up in a wave of white political dudes making stuff up to fit their narrative, satire could reveal a new perspective: what the people being swept up have to say rather than the dudes creating the wave.

So, for now, I'm switching off topical comedy. Reality TV is about as real as I can handle and I know that even that's scripted and staged. I know we only see the bits that they want us to see. I don't care. The lie of reality TV is a welcome break from the fake news of real life.

The innocent early days of *Big Brother*, when people got nominated for not doing the dishes, seem a million years ago. Soap operas used to be the place we went for escapist entertainment. Novels. Plays. No harm to head back there for a bit.

As to where satire goes next? I haven't a clue. I can only tell you that I don't think I'll be able to belly-laugh at current affairs till all of this – whatever 'this' is – has blown over. For the moment, I think I'm all *This-Week*-ed and *What Happened Today*-ed out.

15

RAGE-IN AT THE RUDE

'Think globally, act locally.' I said that earlier, didn't I? Right, well I think I'm going to start going after rude people. Why not? I'm already reacting under my breath in passive aggressive whispers, which only churn me up further. It doesn't achieve anything.

Earlier this week, a man rounded a corner. He was moving quickly, with purpose. He had what looked like short planks under one arm, a spirit level too. He was busy. *So busy.* The corner was in a shopping centre, near where the toilets are. Maybe he had been working on the toilets. Maybe he was working elsewhere and had dropped into the toilets for the kind of break we all need; we are only human after all. We leak.

So, while I don't know his reason for barrelling around the corner, I do know that barrel he did, because he barrelled into me. We didn't quite crash. It was a few planks short of a Laurel & Hardy routine. I saw him in the nick of time and arched my body, *Matrix*-style, avoiding sending spirit level and man flying. No one wants to bruise a stranger. Or maybe I'm thick and they do.

I had what I've always naively assumed to be the instinctive reaction: to laugh nervously and say 'Sorry', even though it wasn't my fault. The fault was neither of ours: destiny itself had brought us to that corner at that moment. We both had a right to be there. Nothing really bad happened. Now, I didn't expect to make a new friend out of a near-miss, but nor was I expecting the scowl I got. No apology, no slowing down. In fact, he grunted his displeasure at my very existence at a corner he had clearly intended to barrel around, unimpeded. He passed. I turned. 'OK!' I said, my arms flapping in exasperation (I wasn't carrying planks or a spirit level; I could flap). I carried on into the loos and lurched into a cubicle, muttering to myself.

As I sat on the cool porcelain, fuming (even the cheeks of my arse were hot with rage), I had time to engage in *l'esprit d'escalier* – the imagining in hindsight what you would have said in the earlier moment had you been calm or clever enough. My comeback didn't amount to much: just me tapping him on the shoulder saying, 'Have a lovely day.' Something like that. Passive aggressive, but my say. Something.

But I hadn't said anything, so I used my porcelain time to analyse why the thing made me so heated. After all, maybe he was having a bad day. You can rarely see other people's pain. But then, he didn't afford me the courtesy of that assumption. And I was having the shittest day: anxiety at its peak, not a chance of hiding or dealing with it. Having to be out and about, putting forth a sunny disposition I was finding hard to dredge up. Exhausted at the prospect and the execution of it. Worried about too many things and with no idea how to resolve them. Counting blessings right and left to be able to manage putting one foot in front of the other. *Right, then left. Say it with me. Right, then left.*

It was into that scenario that Mr Spirit Level barrelled, no more deserving of patience or kindness than I am. Only he estimated that I deserved less. As my butt cheeks cooled, it became apparent that my anger stemmed not from this isolated almost-incident, but from the fact that, more and more, manners seem to be being demanded in one direction only. Maybe that's just my perception. Or maybe I'm just tired of trying to see the good in people when they seem to have no interest in doing the same in return. And believe me, I'm well capable of rudeness. I think rudely all the time. If I catch it in myself, I try to apologise and beat myself up about it, but I'm as prone to it as anyone. So maybe it's time to go for it? Why not indulge in a load of rudeness on those days when I'm struggling? Why not just snap back? I'd fecking love to.

Then I remember the un-fashionability of giving-a-shit (remember Chapter 13) and that has almost definitely played a part in this desire. Politeness, courtesy – they're not cool. Maybe we think we're too busy for them?

They require determination. It's hard. No one likes everyone all the time; we even hate ourselves half the time. It must feel kind-of good to take your bad mood out on all and sundry. Maybe I should have gone after that man and said, 'You have a lovely day', with a face on me, just to see his puzzled reaction. Or maybe it's best I left it where I did, letting him off with the benefit of the doubt, leaving me cursing in a toilet, frustrated at a world where even small courtesies don't seem to count any more. There was plenty of toilet paper, mind you. And I hadn't had to queue. And the porcelain was smooth and cool. Head in hands, I shut my eyes and mutter to myself to remember: *I'm #blessed.*

16

I'VE GOT NOTHING

I dunno, lads. I told you: I definitely haven't got anything figured out. I'm only trying to give you all a laugh, or at least to try to help you process The Shitness, like me. It seems less and less useful to add to the chorus of bleakness. Every week it seems to get harder to know what to say. There are no words to describe the atrocities happening all over the world. There's no doubt that it hurts more when it's somewhere familiar to you. Somewhere close, somewhere that feels almost like home.

Like Barcelona. Or London. Even Las Vegas. Not that that's to ignore horrific occurrences in the Middle East or elsewhere. Not that we're immune to those. But these are cities where friends have been, or maybe you've cousins there, it could have been them. Could have been you. The bombing of an Ariana Grande concert in Manchester in 2017, for example, was particularly brutal. The targeting of innocent young people – kids who haven't harmed anyone, their lives and dreams ahead of them and stars in their eyes – it's just horrible. There are no words. Except *hatred*, maybe. That the perpetrator was motivated by hate is clear.

But what of the rest of it? The toxicity that seems to have been swirling around us this last while?

I'm thinking of those who not only use this type of event for their own gain, but work hard to whip up hate wherever they go. To keep it and themselves in the news. Let's not use their names. That's all they seem to want.

When it comes to hope, I'm finding it hard to dredge mine up from wherever it has sunk to right now. It's never easy to focus on putting positivity out there, almost impossible when we feel empty. And is there even any point?

WAIT! Of course there's a point to hoping, there always is and the swift response of people to these atrocities should be our first inspiration. Many cities manage not to let even the most horrific incident divide them. They make tea, give blood, offer phones and blankets and lifts, either in person or on social media; it would melt even the stoniest heart. It's too easy, in the aftermath of such events, to believe that hardening your heart might be a valid survival choice. It's not a useful way to think, but toughing up and checking out can seem really tempting.

We can't do that. We just can't. But it's not enough to say everything will be all right in the end, when for some, the worst has already happened. So, what option do we have? Where to, when it seems that love alone might not conquer all?

Action. Yep, that old chestnut. That's what we have. That's the option we must choose now. The only thing worse than a hardened heart is to be half-hearted.

Ah, lads! I've got nothing! But it sure does feel like posting inspirational quotes gets us nowhere unless we're also doing something practical. Even starting small, maybe by acknowledging how lucky we are (*There is plenty of toilet paper … And the porcelain is smooth and cool …*), especially if we're not the targets of bigotry, and we then begin to listen carefully to those who are. Maybe we could help to remove offensive graffiti. Choose not to buy inciteful or bigoted material. Switch off hatemongers booked for your telly or radio 'entertainment'. They're not gas. Really. That stuff creeps out into people's real lives. I'm trying not to re-post it – even in outrage. It's our outrage that fuels them. Tell the bookers why you switched off. *Lies and discrimination are hilarious!* surely can't be where we live now, lies rewarded with fame and cold, hard cash.

So while I'm most angry at the perpetrators of atrocities, some responsibility lies with this sort of global chess being played with real people as the pieces. I'm angry at the media for giving platforms to hatred. I'm angry at all of us for giving them sales and listening figures and clicks.

We've all contributed. Maybe we can help to make it stop.

Please don't @ me about free speech if what you really intend is to broaden the platform for those who want to keep it from others. Please don't tell people that they're fighting-for-rights wrong, because you feel immune. Please don't defend terrible behaviour when you'll never be the target of what it's whipping up.

Lads, I don't have any answers. These violent attacks expose the best and worst in people. We might not be able to reach those in power, or those planning the next atrocity. But maybe we can reach those around us. There aren't enough cups of tea to heal the world's wounds – it's hard to see how even time will do it – but tea might be a good place to start. Just switch the bigot on the radio off while you have it.

17

DONKEY POWER: CLIMATE CHANGE ISN'T JUST A PAIN IN THE ASS

Sometimes, in my search for a joke, I tell a small white lie. Sometimes I cast myself as (a bit) thicker than I am (which can be really quite thick) in the hope of a laugh. I love a road-trip, so I regularly nonchalantly describe my potential destruction of the environment. *Haha!* I say, making light of the fact that blazing down the motorway or up some boreen is consuming fossil fuel and munching up the ozone and filling our lungs with emissions. I know there's nothing to make light of there. Of course I care. Of course I do. I used to have nightmares about it – 'cars grinding to a halt … planes falling out of the sky …' – remember? When 'President' Trump yanked America out of climate discussions, a moment arrived when we were all going to have to care a lot harder to make up for whatever he seemed to have planned – things like the *Bring Back Lead* campaign, *Aerosol Your Face Off*, *More Packaging, Please* and *If It Ain't Clogged, Clog It; Clog That Shit Right Up*.

I am torn, so very torn that I'm on the verge of losing sleep about it, like I did during those childhood nightmares. But I do still want the road-trips. I want to sit on blankets, taking in newly discovered vistas (new to me, anyway) and getting rained on up and down the land. I want to see the whole country and meet new people and hear different accents and fight over which *blas* (literally 'flavour', different Irish accents) is best. I want to eat blaas and compare them with farls (like a blaa only more farly – look, I'm not sure what these local bread products really are: it's why I need to go and see for myself; I want to learn) and maybe put them both in a fight refereed by a brown soda cake. I want to swim in the Atlantic and the not-quite-so-Atlantic and try all the newly branded 'Ways' and 'Trails' that used to be simply called 'The Road'.

But how I am going to do that without emitting exhaust fumes and depleting the world's fossil fuel stores? I'm not in the league of being able to afford a snazzy new electric car, though someday, someday, I will and then you'll know I've made it. Even if I had one today, where I live there's no garage so where would I recharge it? I'd have to drive it upstairs every night and plug it in next to my phone. Not a great space-saver. Not sure it'd work.

I guess there are alternatives. I could cycle round the country. I did a lot of that in my twenties and although I had very finely toned calves and thighs, there wasn't a bodily crevice untroubled by a chafe or blister. Even if you're very strong (and I'm not that strong), panniers can only hold a certain amount of tent and clothes. It's very hard to bring the dog along on anything other than a short hop. I've seen the way people look at pet owners who get bike-sidecars for their kids and dogs. You look at them funny. You do. You don't go, 'Ahhh, look there's someone who loves their kid/dog *and* the environment', you give them withering looks usually reserved for mad scientists and evangelical leaflet pushers. Even though all they're pushing is a bike.

I could go the old donkey and cart route. Growing up in the country, we had a donkey at one point. I know how to do the hitching. But that's the easy part. The not-so-easy part is convincing a donkey that he or she would like to take part in the cart operation in the first place. They mostly want to eat grass, hang out with other donkeys or cows, or whatever, and come up with donkey schemes. (Have you looked in their eyes? They're cute, but there are schemes going on, for sure.) Then, again, we're back to where I'd keep a donkey. It needs recharging, just like an electric car. It'd also have to be up in the bedroom, next to the phone charger, with the additional need for some kind of hay and water system. Plus a poop-collection device. Not as simple as it sounds, is it?

Of course, the boffins are probably working on some alternative. Aren't they? Not 'getting the rural bus routes reinstated and maybe extending the train lines'. No, no. Nothing so sensible. I'm sure the boffins are working on hot-air balloons which can only be operated by the more loquacious, using gas from their own excess words. Or electric wheelbarrows: fully rechargeable and easier to get upstairs than a car, with plenty of room for the shopping. Or maybe they're developing manure-powered motor homes: I'm pretty sure a version of this already exists, they just have to prioritise getting rid of the smell.

I don't want to ruin the environment, but sometimes I do find myself evilly parking that thought in favour of parking the car wherever I want to go, under my own steam. If only my own steam could actually propel me there. Then maybe my conscience would be as clean as I'd like the environment to be.

18

A DAY IN THE LIFE IN MY BUNKER — ON PRESCIENCE

Another note from the future.

I never said I was wise. In fact, as previously clarified, I'm definitely not. I'm thick. Just like the rest of you, I couldn't see the future. But even I'm surprised at the amount of things I got right once The Shitness began. You remember, back in 2017, when swearing was suddenly allowed on the News because there was no other way to accurately describe the planet's descent into Shitness? Of course, that was when we still had News. Before News (even Murdoch's NEWS!) was banned. But here in the bunker we try to rise above all that kind of detail and make the best of things.

Originally, as you know, the bunker was started in 2016 and ultimately used for Secret Feminazi meetings but, eventually, we had to broaden access out.[1] Digging wasn't easy – I lived in a building where the garden (remember gardens?) was shared between eight flats, so I really had to hold my ground against other residents and the management company who didn't want a big hole out the back. To think they were worried I'd mess up the water pipes! Sure, we all have free water now, as you know. Too much of it, says you! 'Cos it's everywhere. Keeping it out of the bunker ended up being the biggest structural problem. But

---

1   For more on Secret Feminazi meetings see Chapter 52: 'Dear Fellow Feminazis'.

it's dug now, completed, and many of those only-slightly-damp neighbours are delighted with me.

I even had the foresight to bring a karaoke machine in. Not that I had one lying around; it's the only thing I grabbed during the Flood Looting of 2019. I'd had my eye on it for months. Eventually I just smashed the window of the electrical shop and it floated right into my hands. Now it's in the bunker and the long evenings fly by, so long as you get the song you want. It's best to put your name down the week before.

Not that we really count weeks now the seasons are gone. There's just that one long season now, known as The Soggy. It's good that the media over the last few years has prepared us for these times with the constant dread: 'How safe is your house?', 'Are your thighs out of control?', 'Is your bike/dog/baby where you left it?' Fear, contrarians and made-up facts, it turns out, were a gift all along; they were building up our resistance. If only we'd known it. At the time we took them to be tedious shitelarks. Intellectual empty-barrels.

Now we can forget such heady disagreement, because truth has been limited to what you can actually see, hear, smell or touch. *Is it raining outside? Do we have any fig rolls? Are there any ice-caps left? Can you swim?* Nothing more tedious is considered. It's great that the internet doesn't exist any more because some of our lads used to take refuge in going round in circles on there. Do you remember? Here, offline, in my bunker, it's easier to challenge them. It doesn't matter how we *feel* about us having run out of fig rolls, or the *concept* of running out of fig rolls, we just have. They can try to argue everything from my being biscuit-blind, to fig rolls never having existed at all, but they shut up, right quick, when you show them the empty tin. And when they remember that they loved fig rolls too and now the last remaining person who knew how they got the figs in there has died, all they're left with is the rest of us.

Ditching pointless bickering means we get a lot more benefit from sleep. I say 'we' from experience: you always know if someone's awake at night. Only one room in the bunker.

It's no utopia: of course we don't always agree. But here in my bunker, debating is banned. Not discussion; discussion is what we do rather than watch NEWS! all day, now that NEWS! is gone. Discussion is great. They had simply forgotten how to do it. They only knew how to back themselves into a corner, pointlessly trying to trip people up. The bunker's too small for that, and we've too many other important things to do. Like trying to stay fit, training for whatever disaster's next.

I've made a poster: *Sneering is frowned upon*. Sneering presumes a kind of bored superiority we don't have time for here. The punishment for sneering is having to chalk up today's inspirational quote all over the ceiling of the bunker, hundreds of times. Inspirational quotes drive everyone to distraction, so this is very effective. Nobody wants to read inspirational quotes, all day, upside down, scrawled by their own hand. But we only go in this hard when we really need to make our point.

Encouraged by my uncanny and surprising propensity to get predictions right, I've taken up doing readings. Not Tarot, or anything like that: I read faces, toe-nail clippings, people's breath on the days where it's warm enough for The Soggy to steam. I'm not sure if my visions are correct, but that's hardly the point. I clearly have a gift I've been denying. The surest path is for me to let it out.

I do get a strong sense of how things will have to be. We need to start softening again, starting at our hardened edges and working our way in. Hardened hearts might feel like they protect, but here in the bunker, with hindsight, we see that that's the worst thing that can happen to a heart.

Here are some of our daily softening activities: calling each other eejits; swearing, to get it out of our systems; giving each other a puck in the arm so we remember things actually hurt *if they happen to us*; letting someone have a lie-in the day after they've done Water Watch (to make sure we don't all drown in our sleep).

Inaction is unthinkable. No more armchair commentators: we haven't banned them, of course not. But armchairs are not allowed in the bunker. I must admit, the last dry day we had, when we burned all the leather ones in the middle of Croke Park, is a day that'll live long in my memory. The acrid smoke burned my lungs but the flames lit my face and warmed my softening heart.

Kindness rules in this bunker. Unashamed. Proud. Don't take it for a bunker of fools – you underestimate kindness at your peril. Kindness is about shouting, even pushing back. It's about standing up for your buddies, or people you don't know, when bad shit happens to them. Kindness and courage are interchangeable here in the bunker. If you're not brave enough to be kind, well, we won't throw you out or anything, but we might not let you have your pick in karaoke. Only the crap songs will be left. It might be wise to make sure you get the song you want.

Anger is an energy, but kindness is a generator. And we need something to power the karaoke machine.

MODERN LIVING
FOR THE
MODERN IRE-LANDER

19

TARA FLYNN:
SEEKING EMPLOYMENT

Intermission –
I don't know about you, but I'm relieved to leave the Shitness behind
for a bit and talk about life in our country today. So, on a lighter note:
unemployment.

Look, I haven't worked in a while. Scratch that, I work most days.
What I mean is, I haven't had *paid* work in a while. And I'm not
gonna lie, I'm scared. If fear isn't enough to give you ire, I'm not
sure what is.

Sometimes God closes a door, then closes another door, puts
bars on the windows, stuffs up the chimney and says, 'There ya go,
now, deal with that.' You know you'll get out somehow: I mean,
there might be a hurricane and the gable wall might come down.
It's just that you can't see it yet. You have to sit tight. You have to
be ready for when things change; ideas to hand, ability to pounce.
Opportunity plus preparedness = luck. Isn't that the formula?

I have no formal training in anything other than what I've been
working at since I was twenty, and retraining in your late forties
is a very different proposition than it might have been a decade or
two before. Ten years ago, I'd just moved to London. I started again
from scratch then, so I know what I'm talking about. It's a good
thing to do. But you can't keep doing it.

Or can you? Maybe that's just how things work, these days. Maybe I've been approaching this all wrong. Maybe there are already new

career opportunities open to me from within my skill-set. Maybe I have talents not currently being used that I should be focusing on?

I mean, I sing: I could do one of those cruises people go on when loved ones die. I could sing ancient ballads that people find new love to. Maybe my 'Careless Whisper' will lead to someone's first second-time-around kiss. I wouldn't just be a singer; I would be a mender of hearts. Not because my voice is all that, but because we're out in the middle of the sea and I know all the words to George Michael's magnum opus.

Actually, I know the words to almost every eighties song ever written. If this is ever the category in your pub quiz, I will come round and help out. For money.

I am very flexible in the hamstrings. I could go round to people's houses when they drop things and pick them up. 'You didn't even bend your knees!' they'd say, popping their engagement rings back on. 'Don't need to, ma'am. Don't need to,' I'd say, taking my straight-legged leave, pausing only to collect my moolah and leaving a sense of wonder behind me. (No, I don't mean a fart.)

Speaking of senses (ahem), I have no sense of smell. Really, I don't. I fell off a gate when I was little and there's a bump on my head and they think that's why I don't have one. (Explains a lot else, says you.) It puts me at an advantage in odorous situations. I could be sent in to cheesemongers' where the fridge has died, or to silage-adjacent crime scenes to help out. Unperturbed by the scent and having the hand that other people use to pinch their nostrils free, I would be able to relay details to experts via a GoPro. If they were on site, they'd waste valuable time saying 'Ew!' and that; I'd get straight into collecting forensic evidence or clearing cheese debris with a solution of bicarbonate of soda.

I love to pet animals. I would be happy to do that for yours, even if they're stinky (see above).

I believe that, even though I have been to very few spas, I have a nose for them (despite the above). I would give heavy consideration to reviewing spas at home or abroad. They can be expensive, so this is a vital service. I wouldn't want people wasting their money on a duff one. I would pay particular attention to cleanliness (by visual inspection), towel fluffiness and not-too-talkativeness of therapists. This is what the people want and I'm willing to give it to them for a fee and two large fistfuls of free tiny products.

I would be delighted to take a €250K advance to write a book of bad ideas I only half believe in *because controversy*. Muddening pays, right? I might not be able to sleep at night but I have storage heating and have you seen those winter bills?

I am a great wall painter so long as someone else does the edges/finicky bits. If you know someone who is good at these, we can form a team and go around in a van, singing eighties tunes and getting shit done. Getting shit painted, anyway.

I am a terrible cook. I could pretend to be a caterer and then no matter how bad the host is, they could save the day just by doing sandwiches. It would be a conversation starter too, and everyone loves a conversation at a wedding/funeral/Eurovision gathering.

Something to do with coffee. Anything. I have a problem.

Perhaps my most successful proposal would be an advice service. I keep saying I don't really have any to offer, but actually I've messed up a lot. I'm constantly trying to extricate myself from the results of bad decisions. That must count for something. So what I can offer is a list of things which I know, from experience, *do not work*. As with all my services (except maybe the pet-petting), I'd have to charge for it, but even a coffee voucher as payment would be nice. Once the caffeine hits my bloodstream, maybe I'll start having some good ideas and advice for myself.

20

LIKE THE FIRST DAY OF SCHOOL, ALL OVER AGAIN

Nobody likes change. Definitely not me. I once cried when an old washing machine gave up the ghost and needed replacing. Change sets us on edge. We can't find our stuff and we're not even sure where we're supposed to put ourselves. Here? Or here? It's like the first day of school all over again.

The first day of school is such a giant landmark of excitement and turbulence, most people never forget it. Everything's a negotiation. Am I allowed to play with the bottle-caps-in-sand (a truly magical play area) when I want, or do I have to wait? Is the yard a purely breaktime thing, or can I go there for a think when ABCs get too hard? Will I be punished for thinking for myself, or praised for my moxie like a floppy-capped urchin in a film? There are way more chairs than at home – why can't we sit where we like? And what if I do something bold and have to go to my room? My room is miles away. So many questions. So many new faces, eyes all on you. But at least that first day is over.

Except it isn't. There's always a way to churn up your world, and your stomach, and scare the living shite out of yourself. No better man than life for that. New jobs, new towns, constant reinvention and retraining, technology you have to keep up with or count yourself out of any kind of social or work-life, accidents and – I'm sorry to have to say it – death. Terrifying, isn't it?

It's been quite a while since I was four; I really thought I'd be well past all this by now. Don't tell four-year-old me, but it turns out you're never too old and grown-up for fear of change. Some-times it's a motivator: the fear makes you tough it out and work harder. 'I know what I'm doing!' you say to people's faces, even if they haven't asked. You say it even though your heart is pounding and you feel like a fraud ... more than anything you don't want to be that.

For the next few weeks I'm in London for work and it's the first day of school all over again. I found a gym and signed up for a pre-work class. Laid out my trainers and everything the night before. Made sure I had my lunch money. On the first morning I left early – much too early – to make sure I really did know the way there. There was a PIN to get into the gym, and of course I pani-cked and got my backpack caught in the rotating door. All eyes on me and sweating already, I had to ask where the changing rooms were and blush my way to a locker (can we use just any locker?). I went up three flights of stairs to where the class was being held and waited. No one was coming. For what seemed like hours, nobody came, but then I realised my over-zealous earliness was to blame. Once everyone else arrived, all I had to deal with was screaming self-doubt. I'd be the weakest person there; the others would twirl super-heavy barbells (which, it turned out, were all the rage) above their heads on their pinky fingers while I struggled in a corner to put the weights on the bar and get started. They would laugh at me. I would suck.

One not-too-sucky hour later, not yet 9 a.m. and I still had the new job and a whole lot of unfamiliarity ahead, with even more at stake: I'd suck, they would laugh at me, and on top of it all I'd be fired by the end of the first day. (It's a lot harder to get fired from the gym.) But one week later that still hadn't happened. In fact, I got to the end of the whole job without a firing. We even got an extension! A delay on the next bit of change! Phew. No matter what age you are, no matter how much you talk yourself down, it's hard to shake that new-girl feeling.

***

When I first wrote this piece, I couldn't stop thinking about that week's other new boys and girls: tiny little new TDs, fresh from a general election that had taken ages, shining their shoes and counting their lunch money (which we left out for them). First day in their new job, I couldn't see them being nervous of anything, the neck on them. But many of them are human, surely they must be nervous? Sometimes? Their whole *raison d'être* is to *not* show fear, so do they ever worry about where to sit? Or whether they'll be fired? Is there any voice in their head at all?

They should know this: they might feel like they have the staff-room keys, but we're really the teachers. They're on continuous assessment, we're all eyes on them, and the tests from now on are going to be marked very hard. We're in a bad mood, no messing. Or there'll be no bottle-caps-in-sand for them.

21

THIS IS PANTS
— ON BEING 'BORED'

It's weird going to someone's house for the first time. You have to find it first. That's less tricky since they put GPS on all the phones so they know where we are because, as a nice side-effect, we know where we are most of the time too. But finding the place is only the start of the weirdness.

You have to break the ice with the person, who you probably don't know very well. If you do know them well, why has it taken them so long to invite you round? Might it be time you consider recalibrating your personality? You have to remember not to touch stuff. Best take your shoes off, just in case. (Best wear brand new socks too.) Did you bring a small gift? You should have brought a small gift. 'Your place is lovely!' you say, usually true, so you mentally burn your own place down and redecorate from scratch.

Then, especially if you're a woman, there's the whole added frisson of whether you'll make it out again, on the *outside* of a bin-bag. Being on the outside of one is, obviously, the goal. This is something that every single woman in the world tries to laugh off before going into a new place. 'I'm being such an eejit!' she chuckles, as she checks under her host's sink for too-much cleaning equipment. 'Ha ha ha!' she says as they come back from the loo and she tries to pretend she hasn't run a quick background check via Interpol. By which I mean Google-ing them and anyone who might know them on Facebook. Or are they a loner? You know, the kind of fella who 'keeps himself to himself'? Voted 'most likely in his class to make headlines for the wrong reasons'?

All this went through my mind as I searched for someone's house in North London last week. She's a producer and had offered her place up for an interview. She and other colleagues and I had all been back and forth on the phone, so it was clearly above board. But as I turned onto her street, I got a massive feeling of déja vu. I'd been here before. Why had I been here before? I'd never been here befo…

It dawned on me. A guy I had dated for a couple of months about a million years ago lived only a block away. This wasn't his street and I was coming from the opposite direction, so I was a bit turned around and that's why I didn't recognise it straight away.

But the corner shop, pubs and gardens tugged at something in my brain until it all came rushing back. It was not a welcome rush. Christ, that was grim.

I'd only been to his place about three times during the whole thing. I say 'thing': it wasn't a relationship, or a romance, but nor was it neither. It was a 'thing'. The first time he had a friend there when I arrived, as if to say, 'I'm not going to murder you! Or, if I am, I have help, so at least it'll be quick!' He had cooked for the three of us, which also made murder a bit less likely: why create the extra washing up? The second time, there was no friend, no cooking. And the third, we were broken up and trying to be friends. Which, reader, was a DISASTER. Why? He had a catchphrase, and that catchphrase was 'I'm bored.'

This man worked two jobs, had a ton of friends, a hobby about which he was (supposedly) passionate, yet declared himself constantly bored. I didn't see it right away, but eventually he'd told me so often I couldn't miss it. His quiet moods weren't quiet, they were judgemental; everyone bar him was boring. His movements weren't laid back, they were borderline inert. I remember some wise aul wan' telling me when I was little that 'bored people are boring people' and it turns out she was right. He was dull. Handsome, smart, but dull as dishwater. Which he wouldn't have been – at all – if he hadn't talked *ad nauseum* about how dull everyone and everything else was.

Does a boredness epidemic have us in its grip? Do we feel entitled to be stimulated all the time? We seem to believe happiness lies in constant activity, activity we don't have to hand right now, to drive ourselves. Other people are supposed to entertain us and they're substandard if they don't. They're accessories to our self-centred existence. Content. (Not content as in 'happy' but content as in 'stuff' or 'filler'.) We seem to have found ourselves in a zone where thinking is 'doing nothing' and an uneventful day is a bad one. (Albeit one in which, perhaps, you've avoided all manner of awful – you're alive, aren't you? But no one seems to realise that.) Information and services are supposed to be *right now*, or they're 'slow'. There's an arrogance to it, our old pal entitlement, suggesting your busy mind is quicker than the rest. But is it? I'm not so sure.

In any event here I was, back on, or near, Boring Street and the memories weren't good. But then I remembered the last contact we'd had. He'd left underpants at my place – just the one pair – and these forgotten boxers had been driving me crazy. I didn't want to think about him any more, so holding on to them was out of the question, but something kept me from tossing them. Maybe there was some craic to be had.

I washed the boxers, folded them, wrapped them in brown paper, nipped down to the post office and sent them off to his address. I'll never know if he got them. I can only imagine his reaction. (Bored, probably.) But as I walked down, or near, Boring Street to my interview – despite the fact that I wasn't sure where I was going and I hadn't even brought a present – man, how I laughed.

22

BURNOUT

I've always tried to do things right. Even if self-wrong-teousness ends up getting the better of me, half-arsing seems to me such a waste of your own and everyone else's time. Apart, that is, from folding laundry. Oh, I'll happily skimp on that shit. I can slam-dunk a creased but clean top into an open drawer from across a room and I'm proud of it. I live with an obsessive (and very talented) folder; part of me is simply restoring balance. But part of it is undeniably, 'It's clean. My work here is done.' In this instance I have none of my usual desire to follow through, to help the laundry reach a dignified end to its cycle. I'll be wearing the thing again soon, for goodness' sake, everybody chill out. If only I could apply a pinch of my attitude to crumpled clothing to everything else.

'Give it one more pass,' my conscience will say, sometimes in the middle of the night. 'If you do it right now, you'll have free time tomorrow.' But of course, I won't. I'll fill that extra time with research or admin, telling myself I'm making space for more crea-tive work when the muse shows up. And even if the muse doesn't show up, even if I'm not being paid for a project, I will be there at my desk rat-tat-tatting out ideas because it's my job. If I don't commit, who will? When I travel, I take work with me, or make sure to take a class I couldn't take at home. Why waste the oppor-tunity to learn?

Other freelancers will recognise this feeling, a big chunk of which is – DUH – fear. Ugh. *That* guy. *If I don't work hard enough, someone else will take the spot. If this piece isn't as good as it can be, I'm a failure. And not just this piece/play/show: it has to generate more*

work. What if I don't even get paid? Time is running out, hurry, hurry!
The problem then, though, is there are no days off. There can't be.
The problem then is burnout.

I have recently come dangerously close to burning out. It has
been no fun at all, I can tell you.

This hasn't just been down to workaholism or drive, there's been
emotional burnout too. Add financial woes into the mix for the
craic; most of us know about those. Daily pummellings from self-
righteous idiots who think it's acceptable to pass judgement on
strangers' lives (of course, I mean mine) didn't help either. They
don't care what response their hateful actions trigger. Actually, they
probably do care: having people feel like shit and shut the hell up
is seemingly exactly what they want. Well, ultimately their opinion
is irrelevant so while they might wind me, they can't wound. But
throw in a few thinly veiled threats and Bingo! We have a full
house – a scenario capable of making you stress-drunk quicker
than neat brandy. For a few weeks there, my heart was audibly
pounding, adrenaline surging in and out like the tide: who could
possibly sleep with all that going on? In other words, I was mostly
awake.

That led to not having any energy. I couldn't exercise. I couldn't
socialise and gigs were taking every last resource to get to, let alone
do.

So I took my own advice and did something – that 'something'
being less. I pared back my time online, only popping on when I
felt it was important, or conversely for a break and some fun. I
got up earlier to work on a longer, on-spec project, giving it my
all while still leaving time to walk the dog. I pulled out of a few
unpaid things and turned down some requests for favours – that
was really hard, but, as the husk I was becoming, I'd have been
no good to them anyway. I asked the evil HeadStuff bosses for

a couple of weeks off. Took a sabbatical from Dublin Comedy Improv. And guess what? I booked a holiday. An actual holiday, where laptops are banned. (By me. It's not a creepy camp or anything.) Where there will be sunshine and time to talk and reading and eating and sleeping. What a treat. Who do I think I am, Liberace? If not him, somebody equally fancy. I know how lucky I am that I can manage it.

Booking it, taking that time, I felt instantly better. Ideas started flowing again, catching up with people was back on the cards. The days don't feel quite the same gargantuan effort any more. I still have my old-school paper notebook on the go in case ideas pop into my cooling brain, but I'm getting better at jotting them down and shutting it again. Not having a boiling brain feels so good.

So if the burnout has passed, why share this? Because you'll never see burnout on Instagram. But it's out there, happening to loads of us. Let me be your cautionary tale. Go and make yourself a cup of tea and go outside and look up at the sky. I mean it. Even if it's raining.

And the laundry? It can sit on the clothes horse for another day. Probably best to make sure it's really, really dry, anyway. How else can you make sure it creases up just right?

23

PEACE AND QUIET

Recently I stayed somewhere really quiet. It wasn't even a holiday it was just really quiet: no TV, no nothing. Just peace and quiet. The air was clean and all you could hear from outside was the bleating of sheep and the hum of the odd car as it wound its way slowly up the hill. Slowly was the only way anything got done: the WiFi was sluggish, the gradient steep; it was wonderful. I breathed in, breathed out. It did my heart good. My head stopped buzzing (it's either this or boiling) for a minute and there was stillness and I was able to just switch off and …

WHO AM I KIDDING? Me? No way. Not all the way. I've been trying for years and it's never happened. Holidays are good: I can slow down a bit and live in the moment, a bit. But there are too many problems to solve and let's be honest, solving things can be a buzz.

Like many stressed Westerners (Stresserners?) I've done yoga for years and I used to beat myself up about how I couldn't get my head to empty as others in class seemed able to. They would boast about how much lighter they felt, metaphorical weights lifted off their shoulders. Unfurrowed brows. Clean slates. A mindful practice like yoga probably offers me more calm than is naturally available to me but I can't help cheating: some of my best ideas come when tied up like a pretzel, when I'm supposed to be letting those ideas glide by, or putting my thoughts in a bubble and letting them float away. The having time to think only gets me thinking all the more:

- *My worries are tied to a kite and it's flying away, super-high? What if it goes into a jet-engine and brings down a plane? How would I live with the guilt?*

- *I'm by a lake and the water is gently lapping at the shore? Who's minding my stuff? Where are my keys? Is anybody pervy nearby – is it safe to have my eyes closed all the way out here?*

- *I'm in a peaceful, white space? WHY? Is it a cell? What did I do? What's the food like? Does anyone have the WiFi password? And who's coming to let me out?*

So, you see, emptying my head completely of future and past has never been an option for me. There's too much imagining to do. *Watch it back, impartially, like a movie?* Ha! You've never seen me watch movies. I silently wriggle and squirm with emotion if I'm in public; if I'm at home, it's a running commentary, aloud. 'Why would he do that, the feckin' eejit?!' Of course, we're particularly judgemental of ourselves, so watching myself back would never be an impartial experience. To me, I'm a feckin' eejit all the time. I would want to hurl stuff at the make-believe meditation screen. This energy isn't exactly blissful.

I went to India, a land for centuries synonymous with quests for inner peace (if you can ignore the odd bitta violent colonialism). Obviously, as I was the one going, my own head and thoughts still attached, I had no such high peaceful hopes for myself. But I learned a lot about peace and who gets to have it. I learned things I already knew, but it slaps you when you see it: like, how really very rich and lucky we are, even in Ireland, with our running water and all the rest of it. Like, for all the systemic misogyny in our own country, Ireland is a relatively safe place. Like, there is probably nowhere scarier or more beautiful or exciting on Earth than India.

It's practically impossible to find a quiet corner there and that's most likely the reason why it's where yoga was born. Between the constant burr of mopeds and tuk tuks, the honking horns of the breadmen's pushbikes, and dogs and other creatures chatting loudly to each other as it gets dark, or monkeys landing on the roof, it's a miracle anyone switches off, ever, at all. Not to mention the fact that, if it does get quiet, there still might be snakes. I was a comfortable, privileged tourist, but I was on edge the whole time – which, given that I was travelling alone, was probably a pretty smart state for me to be in. I loved the place. I was terrified of it. I really want to go back. But inner peace I did not find.

What you realise in a place where extreme poverty and hardship are the daily norm is what a luxury the very concept of peace is. How it isn't something we all get, let alone something we're owed. You want to sit cross-legged on a beach and leave your phone behind? Me too. It's good to remind ourselves that that means we're not at immediate risk and that we have food in the fridge, that we *have* a fridge and that we're not having to dig in the ground for water. Let's put that in our peace pipes and smoke it.

I thought about a moving meditation to do on myself: the Cop-On Slap. It's where I slap myself in the face and remember that, as stressed as I am, as anxious as I get, I can always do with getting a grip. Peace might not be attainable, but hopefully perspective is.

24

WHAT I WANT

It's said that framing ambitions in the negative is no good. Even in Modern Ire-land, where, as the name suggests, we still love a good moan. Instead you're supposed to form a positive list of your wants. For example, you mustn't say 'I DON'T WANT to spend today letting self-doubt curl me into a *Judge Judy*-watching lump on the couch.' *I WANT*, you must say. *I NEED*. And *I AM GONNA GET*. You make the positive list and then you go for it, apparently, and if good things don't happen then you're just not going for them hard enough. You don't have enough self-belief, you see, so it's your fault. I don't know about you, but I find self-blame to be a really useful motivational tool. NOT. It means I'm not only hobbled by the idea that the world might judge me, I have proof that someone *is* actually, right now, judging me: *me*. I am such a dick sometimes.

That agreed, there might be a kernel of truth in the positive framing of wants and needs. (I like my truth in kernels. I like that truth might one day become popcorn.)

So, I've decided to share my own list with you. Of course, when I'm not writing this list out longhand on the most beautiful paper I can find and then sending it to myself in the post (I must act surprised when it arrives; it has been sent by some wise and gentle benefactor), I'm whispering it aloud into my Zoom recorder to play back in the background of whatever I'll be doing later. Washing the dishes? Why would I waste such an activity by not self-improving? If a dish can have scum soaped off it, why can't I soap off my emotional scum? Or walking the dog, why wouldn't I listen to myself whispering *You Go, Me* platitudes? The negative chatter in my head can always use company – or, in this case, competition.

It's possible I haven't been thinking big enough. So, I'm planning a new way to frame my wants – to really put them out there in the physical world. I'm going to go deep into the woods and find the biggest, oldest oak tree I can, chainsaw it down, drag it back to where I live (this may take some days) and then begin lovingly carving my wishes into its bark. When I'm done (and only when I've put every wish and dream on there) I'll take a few days off from working to begin the laborious-but-worth-it task of hauling the carved trunk to a large body of water and setting it on fire: a kind of Viking funeral for my lack of self-belief. Believe you me IT'S GONNA WORK.

Here are the wants I will carve:

- I want to live to be 110. I reckon, by then, I might have just about written everything down that I need to. The extensive carving might eat into writing time now and then but, again, it'll be worth it. I'm gonna be 110 but still supple and bendy and ailment-free. I want to die, when I die, with only minutes' notice and doing something I love. Like carving.

- I want to get paid a million euro for everything I do. Per job, like. No more door-splits, unless they're a million euro. And there'll be no below a million euro contracts. This way I might pay off my mortgage before I'm 110 and die while carving.

- I want to hand over the world's decision-making to animals. Not just cute, domestic animals, but wildcats, jungle beasts, deep sea eyeless fish: their instincts can't be worse than the incredible fucking eejitry that's taken hold of the planet's humans. Plus, it would mean that – instead of a shitfest of misery – the nightly News would look a lot more like *Planet Earth*, which can only be an improvement. Some of us will get eaten under the new furry, scaly regime, but it looks like we're going to be swallowed whole under the current one anyway, so we may as well be involved in some high speed cheetah chases before we go. So majestic.

- I want all religions to be shmooshed into one super-religion called *You Wha'? You Wha'?* is what you'd say whenever someone else expounds a belief you can't get on board with. You simply say *You Wha'?* and that's all the reaction you're allowed. You say it and move on. We get it, you don't agree. No bombing anyone or giving withering stares. *You Wha'?* is both the most disdainful and loving religion there's ever been. I know this can work.

- I want more chocolate. Dark, non-dairy, preferably mint.

And that's my list. As you can see, there's a lot of unselfishness and world betterment going on there, so long as I get a million euro and some chocolate. If I were us, I'd see that I got it.

25

THE TWISTY ROAD LESS TRAVELLED

Here's where I have to self-wrong-teously park my nightmare-induced environmentalism. I need to talk about cars and my love of them. I couldn't drive until my thirties, which was the first time I was able to afford to run a car. Before that, I was a strictly bike and bus person. Then, when I moved to London I added the Tube into the mix. I sold the car to help fund the move and only rented one once the whole five years I lived in the UK, to go to a wedding.

When I moved back to Ireland, I was still doing comedy gigs around the country and needed a car for that. We bought a banger from a lovely man in Balbriggan and got every last mile out of it, till it stopped, smoke billowing from the bonnet on the side of the road one rainy day a year later. Before it fully stopped, it stopped a few times 'for no reason'. One of those times was on Tara Street at rush hour. Everyone was shouting at me. A kind man helped me to limp the ailing crock (not me, though I was a bit sweaty) up onto the pavement so some cars could pass. I stood apologetically waving at people shaking their fists at me. But – BUT – I made it onto AA Roadwatch as a congestion problem so it was great for exposure.

After three further car-free years, I have one again. I don't take it for granted. I use it sparingly. But I can't deny that one of the best things about having one is road-trips. Throwing the dog and the husband into it and getting down the country is the best. It doesn't matter where, this country's made to be seen and a car really helps.

Especially now that they're taking all the buses away in a terrible and seemingly unthinking move. So, for the moment, we're lucky enough to have one and getting lost down roads we don't know in this land of ridiculous signposts is one of Ireland's great pleasures.

Some of my happiest childhood memories were in cars. At the risk of sounding like an Enid Blyton book or *Sunday Miscellany*, there'd be flasks packed and eggs hard-boiled and off we'd go. My grandad's jalopy had one of those gear sticks that came out of the dashboard and took up half the car. I might be remembering this wrong, but I think I could see the road beneath my feet. But anyway, off we'd go on an adventure – maybe to the creamery to see other old lads talking about milk and the price of it. Literally. Or to the beach for a swim. Family picnics always seemed to coincide with rainy days and although it's hard to play 'I Spy' with the windows all fogged up with condensation, we gave it a damn good go. 'I spy … something beginning with … C.' (Answer: Condensation.)

There was the night when Mum, Dad, my sister and I borrowed a friend's caravan on a clifftop in Clifden and a storm whipped up, rocking the caravan so hard we were all sure it was about to end up in the Atlantic. So we got dressed and drove a few miles inland and slept in the car.

My first time leaving Ireland was on the car-ferry, when Dad drove us from Cork to Eastbourne for my aunt's wedding. I was only four, but I remember a lot of the drive over. It was a huge deal to be leaving the country. We saw dolphins from the ferry deck. On the way back, both my sister and I had somehow caught measles, so as miserable as I was on the return journey, I'm sure it was no fun at all for our parents: two sick kids and an overnight sailing. Hurrah! They were probably never so happy to park the car and get into the house.

Anyway, all that because this weekend, the fella and I will hopefully do one of those trips. Because he's American, I love showing the place off to him – ire-inducing or not, there's loads of it he hasn't seen and loads I haven't seen for ages or am experiencing for the first time with him. It really *is* so green. It really *is* so lush. It really *is* true that if we got the weather we'd never go anywhere else.

I have to be at the wheel because the American can't understand how anyone drives here. He thinks we're mad to attempt it on twisty former donkey tracks. And maybe we are, but that's how they are and I intend – while I still have a car – to cover as many of those twisty, windy feckers as humanly and vehicularly possible. I'm sure this is playing into the oil barons' hands and possibly contributing to the destruction of the lush greenness over time, but I'm hoping my *car*-bon footprint is low enough to buy me a few road-trips now, for balance. I hope so. I've already filled my flask.

26

IT'S MY BIRTHDAY AND I'LL CRY TO GEORGE MICHAEL IF I WANT TO

It's my birthday!

I know, you're not supposed to say, but fuck it, it's my birthday and I'm already drunk. (I'm not. Or am I?)

It's not a significant one – they're the ones with zeroes in them – but it's significant enough to me. It's my birthday, I'm still here and that's amazing. Phew. (Christ, I hope I don't die after I file this on Friday or this will be a fierce poignant column altogether. If that is the case, please cry tears filled with regret that we didn't spend half enough time hanging out together. I'd have liked that too.)

I was born on 25 June, exactly sixth months after – or before – Christmas, the year of the moon landing. Yes, that long ago. I reckon the astronauts waited for me. I was told when I was little that as the date was 'the opposite' of Christmas, it was a kind of devilish day. (Something to do with *The Omen*. I still check my head for horns periodically, but so far, it's just frizzy hair up there, nothing too bumpy.)

I share the day with those excellent Improv-ers Mike McShane and Phill Jupitus. So there must be something in the date about making stuff up. George Orwell is another astro twin. Yeah, that slouch. And the fact that my favourite day-sharer ever, George Michael, is now gone will probably make me weep copiously into my Prosecco-with-orange-juice-in-it on the day, as I make gentle circuits of the living room to 'Kissing a Fool'.

Speaking of Michaels, on my fortieth birthday Michael Jackson stole my thunder by making it the day after which he wouldn't have any more birthdays. Or any days, really. Everyone was sad, making the end of a nice day in a beer garden a lot more subdued than days in beer gardens are supposed to end up.

Gaudi, Repeal legend Lucy Watmough, Dave from The Umbilical Brothers: we all popped out on this Opposite of Christmas Day, causing our mothers to say, 'Thank flip for that; I couldn't manage the heat any more.' It's good company. I might have to up my birthday game.

I'm hoping for quiet, uneventful ones from now on. I've had a lot of them at this stage but a few stand out. There was the one where we had a party at our house, the year I was to get my first bike. I was buzzing on excitement and sugar. A girl we kind of knew – she didn't even go to school with us in Kinsale – was also buzzing and insisted she get a go on the bike. My bike. My first bike. Before me. And she got it. My parents let her. Christ forgive me, but I'm still hunting the woman down and when I do, I will put her on a stationary bike and make her eat birthday cake for a full day. I know my parents meant it to be a lesson in sharing and the unimportance of material stuff, but it was MY BIKE. MY FIRST BIKE. And someone else had the first go on it. The saddle was sullied. But I'm over it now. (I will find her.)

Some years we took the party to the beach. It was the seventies; we were all about trying new things. An Irish beach party meant packing a lot of sausages and children (some, like me, barely indistinguishable) into about three cars, with roughly six adults on tenterhooks for the three or so hours we spent on the beach as they scanned the horizon for the sight of a child being swept out to sea. Our legs were pure blue (as ever) from the cold and in the pictures we're wearing anoraks, but I feel the defiance shows in our blue legs. Shorts all the way. Because it was the SUMMER. Even when it wasn't. This version of events was probably the hardest for seventies parents because the beach meant distance from sherry – probably the only thing that made the house party option bearable.

I spent one birthday touring a one-woman show. All on my own in a (lovely) dressing room in Galway. I think I went out and got a muffin for breakfast, but I didn't stick a candle in it. I wanted to, though.

The thing is, I love birthdays. The idea of age bothers some people, but when it's actually happening, you don't really notice. You feel the same. You hear people, outside, maybe say something about 'looking good for your age' (unless you're prematurely invisible), or 'still' doing certain things (can anybody still see me?), but it really is in the mind. Until, eventually, it's in the body and immobility beckons. I'm not looking forward to that. I'm afraid of illnesses that could lie ahead. I'm afraid of not being here any more. (Which hopefully hasn't happened between submission and today. Remember to cry if it has.) It's horrible that the hardest bit of most people's lives, physically, is at the end.

But that's why it's important to celebrate. So why limit it to just the one day? Listen, the week of my birthday I'll be having extra fancy coffees the whole week. I'll have more than a few wines. I'll play hookey from work the odd afternoon (which no one will notice if I'm only working for me). I'll probably buy the good kind of toilet paper. I'll give myself the week. A festival, like everyone else does at Glastonbury that weekend, but this one is all about my birthday. My birthstival. If I don't, who will?

I hope you have a happy one.

27

GOALS FOR A NEW YEAR

I've never liked my body – never, ever. It's been with me as long as I can remember and as long as I can remember I've always been hard on it. My attitude's probably not going to change. At least my critique is consistent. My body's changed shape constantly over time, reflecting what's been going on in my life, good and bad, but I've come to realise that I'll never like it. It's not even its fault: it's done nothing but not be like the women in the pictures in magazines, or on stage or screen – and now, as I get older, even as more 'normal' women are better represented, after a certain age they start vanishing too. Vanishing from the stage or screen part is tricky, because that's part of what I do for a job. It can seem like – if you don't break through quite quickly and corner the market in 'character' parts – the prerequisite for an actress is to be willowy, tall and have impossibly big eyes like a fawn so there's less CG work to do post-production. Eyelashes too: I've noticed a trend in filming actresses from above so the camera catches a tear trickling gently out from beneath three-foot lashes, clearly funded by the production so they're determined to get the value for them. That's right, I can even find fault with my scrawny, inadequate eyelashes. And I'm aware that this feeling isn't unique to me.

Given that I'll never love it, the best I can hope for at this stage is to make friends with my body. Be thankful for it when it's in good health, as it mostly is, for now. Well done, body, you're great. I should say that more. I've put you through a lot. So I try to feed it right, I keep an eye on alcohol intake and I work it out whenever I have time. I try every healthy, mobile day to notice: *I'm not in hospital.* This instantly lifts my mood. I don't currently have an illness or injury, bar the asthma for which I'm lucky enough to live in a time and place where I can easily get medication. Age has brought some interesting knee-noises when I stand up too fast, but other than that, my body's been a great, under-appreciated buddy to me.

Next January, however, despite my resolutions to the contrary, I guarantee I will still fall into the trap of the relentless onslaught of 'You're Shit' ads that flood every commercial break for the month. I will still, despite my better judgement, regret every fun thing I ate or drank over Christmas, even though I savoured every second of it. I will internalise the knowledge that I am a failure and only this gym-membership or that anti-cellulite product can save me. I will feel guilty for having a healthy body that goes through seasonal phases, that responds naturally to movement and fuel. I should 'cleanse' (I am dirty), I should 'detox' (I am poison), I should be 'new' (I am useless and old). My brain doesn't believe these messages, but goddamit, after four decades of this shit, some of it's stuck in my heart.

To counter this, my aim will be not to perfect, or sculpt, or punish my body any more. I will try instead to be the friend I want to be to it. Let it do its thing in peace. To distract myself, come time for resolutions, I could always choose completely non-body-related goals instead.

I will become a despot. It seems to be all the rage these days and you get in all the best places, like the White House and restaurants with gold lighting that are particularly flattering. I need all the help I can get.

No selfies in fluorescent lighting. Not out of vanity but so as not to shut down Instagram with the fright and the glare.

I will have my own radio station, broadcasting in secret from within a mountain lair. I will play only eighties hits to which I know the words, and sing along. I know the words to a LOT of eighties hits. There will be a LOT of Bowie and George Michael. This will take up more airtime than you can possibly imagine. There will be no requests, for fear any of them would include 'Stop singing along to eighties hits.' (Being a despot will have many hidden benefits such as these.)

I will contrive to have someone pay me to go on holiday and write about it. (Just in case I'm not asked to review those luxury spas.) Even though despoting will take up a lot of my time and guarantee me an income (everyone else's), I simply couldn't give up doing what I love: going on holiday.

I will find a mainstream publication, programme or website that hasn't had a hilarious racist on for clicks. I know it's hard to believe, but they're out there. I will find them and report back.

I will bring back thatching and weaving and other lost crafts and skills. Like listening. Nobody does that any more. We used to have storytellers – now they'd never get even halfway through the story of Cúchulainn without someone butting in to argue that the story was shit because the seanchaí neglected to mention that #notallmen accidentally kill dogs with sliotars.

That's plenty to be getting on with not only every January, but year-round too. And I didn't even mention Nutribullet once.

28

THE TRIALS AND TRIBULATIONS OF VALENTINE'S DAY

It'd make you sick, wouldn't it?

Oh, I'm sorry – am I wrecking your buzz? Are you having a wuvwy Vawentine's Day? Did you wake up this morning in a sun-drenched room, your partner having lovingly drugged you over-night and put you on a plane to somewhere there's enough sun for drenching? *Surprise!* Was a string quartet hovering close to your pillow, gauging your eyelids for every flicker so they could begin to play 'Spring' from Vivaldi's *Four Seasons* as soon as those precious lids fluttered open? And was their hovering not at all creepy? Was your lover poised with a breakfast tray, champagne flutes and a single rose between his or her teeth? (The 'big' flowers came yes-terday. Remember, you acted surprised.) Were you fed mimosas and Béarnaise-covered morsels and tiny bits of bread, like a loved-up duck? Was there some kind of jewellery hidden in your eggs, a card delivered by a snow-white dove appearing at just the right moment and alighting on your shoulder? And then did you make sweet, sweet love in a sunspot, with the quartet retreating a little too late for it to be strictly comfortable? Was Jamie Dornan in-volved at all? And something to do with chocolate?

I'm exhausted even thinking about such an over-romantic pro-duction and also a bit annoyed, and I'm not sure who to blame. We point at the card companies and say, 'You did this. You made this pink shit happen.' But they're not forcing us into newsagents at gunpoint. Apparently, we want this. We ask for it. Or do we?

The ubiquitous pink is only the start of it. It's an okay colour, I'll give you that, but not the kind you'd want everywhere. It's no purple. Then there are the teddies where there aren't ever supposed to be teddies: flower shops and garages and supermarket tills. Teddies, normally so cute, suddenly seem to be passive aggressively screaming through plate-glass shop windows, 'Take me home or your love will die!' I can't be the only one who hears them scream. Can I?

And as to anonymous admirers, it can't be healthy to encourage people who don't know each other at all well to find out each other's addresses. (Bin bags, remember?) There's that tricky balance between 'Aww, they went to all that effort' and 'They're watching me right now aren't they? They're inside the house.' Far be it from me to judge, but it might be sliiiightly unhealthy emotional territory when we're more disappointed at getting nothing in the post, than relieved at not being stalked.

Over the years, I've had way more shite Valentine's Days than I've had good ones (what, you can tell?) and the day itself still causes me to twitch. In one of life's cruellest economy drives (the explanation I give myself to comfort myself), I was once dumped in the week running up to 14 February. Another year the dumping happened the day after Valentine's, with me having just received the biggest box of chocolates and bouquet of roses anyone had ever seen. I swear, they could be monitored from space and I only wish I could have seen the dumping coming from equally far away. It is profoundly depressing to be lonely in a flat where you can't move for love-flowers, symbolically wilting as the days go by. Insensitive feckers. The chocolates were nice, though. I'd ask where he got them if I hadn't deleted his number on 15 February.

Some of you probably couldn't be bothered about the day either way. Good attitude. Well done. But some of you will wake up alone on the day and the frenzy surrounding it will make you feel shit, even if you're otherwise fine with your own company. I remember that feeling and I'm angry on your behalf. You're not bitter, you're not sad, you're normal. It's them – the try-hard fanciness pink-shit people – they're the ones who aren't normal. So I'm not going to suggest you 'romance yourself' with a long, candlelit bubble-bath, or send yourself a card telling yourself how much you appreciate yourself. Ugh. Have a regular day. Hand-wash your undies. Breathe. This too shall pass.

By no means am I anti-love and romance. At the end of one particularly stressful day, my husband arrived home with a mint chocolate bar. For me. Mint chocolate is my favourite. (You might have noticed.) And once, when we had freshly exchanged keys, I came home from a long journey to find him cooking dinner at mine. Nothing fancy, just dinner, to eat, because I was hungry and tired. Sometimes he gets up quietly in the morning and takes the dog out (not a euphemism) even though he's a much bigger fan of a lie-in than I am. In return? I make sure there are eggs in the fridge – he likes eggs, they're like mint chocolate to him – and bring him back a book or something *Star Wars*-related when I've been away.

But Valentine's Day? We often just ignore it. It's expensive and stressful. Paying that much to queue for dinner or drinks and not be able to have a good old-fashioned bicker in case you 'waste' the occasion isn't our idea of a good time. I don't really think it's anyone's. I wish someone would embroider that on a teddy.

29

CELEBRITY — FROM Z-LIST UP

I was on a bus the other day when another passed. On its side was an ad: a competition to win 'A Celebrity Wedding'. I wondered what it meant. Did you get a well-known person to marry, if you won? Were they nice, or amenable to marriage in the first place? Had they consented? Or did it just mean a wedding like a celebrity would have? Because then it gets more puzzling still.

I think when we say 'celebrity' these days, what we mean is 'lavish' or 'glamorous' or even 'OTT'. Celebrity used to mean someone you saw on MTV or had been in a film or ran a country – although it was usually reserved for the less serious end. Newsreaders were not 'celebrities'. Celebrities were a class of eejit who spent their money on big cars and drugs but actually did have some kind of real talent or cultural contribution to make that meant you couldn't tell them they were eejits. But we're all celebrities now, or are supposed to want to be. That should be shocking; imagine people measuring their own and others' worth by fame. Oh shit. It's here.

In certain jobs (including my own) profile has a direct link to ticket or unit sales and to that end, advertising is important. Plugging – either in an interview or on your own Facebook page – is part of the deal. But recognition in and of itself should be meaningless. It's Modern Ire-land, for God's sake – we all know each other anyway. And in terms of units, there are only three of us. That means you can sell up to three tickets or books maximum; believe me, you're grateful for every single sale, but it's hardly going to keep you in faux fur coats, unless you do a sponsorship deal with a faux fur coat company.

It seems the most cutting insult some people can think of in this fame-zone is: 'You're nothing but a Z-list celebrity.' It makes me laugh for minutes, I tells ya, minutes. Like I know the alphabet! Let alone how the celebrity version works. They don't make an alphabet for where someone like me fits into that system. Is there a minus-alphabet? I might be on that. Maybe. At a push. Luckily, most creative creatures I know don't worry about that system. There's too much work to be doing.

It's clear some people do see fame itself as a career. Not just reality TV stars: anyone trying to carve a niche out of attention. Appearing on TV shows or writing contrarian articles – so contrary! so muddy! – unable to conceal shit-eating grins if they cause any little ripple of controversy.

I have the opposite problem. I want to keep my opinions to myself but when something is genuinely giving me ire I struggle to keep my mouth shut. Then I wonder why detractors pile on. The lads think they've found an opponent; someone who wants to play their attention game. But I suck at it, because I don't get fired up by it; I just get weary. I don't get the kind of ire-erection (irection?) they seem to; I wish I did – it sounds so fun.

So if you think calling me a non-celebrity will put me back in my box, sorry lads, wrong box. When I started doing what I do, there was no fame to be had from it. There was no internet, no chasing likes or shares. You did gigs in pubs to twenty-five people for a door-split. Telly was grand if you got on it but again, here, everyone was already on it. As an actor, most got into the business because they were addicted to stage work, often wishing they could give theatre up – a nice office job would pay more and be much less terrifying – but they were unable. You did what you did because you had to, because you loved it. It just came out that way.

It's weird when someone tries to wield their perception of

your fame as either stick or carrot. You're either *too famous* (i.e. out of touch, elitist, weird) or *not famous enough* (loser, washed up, pathetic). It fascinates me how concerned some people are with the celebrity (or lack thereof, they'll be quick to say) of someone like me, someone they say they've never heard of.

The concept of fame as reward becomes a concern when employers try to pay you in 'exposure'. You know, like ending up on AA Roadwatch. 'There's no money, but you're getting on TV/radio/column inches!' As if that is supposedly the goal in itself; not doing good work and being paid for it, with exposure as an only-sometimes-welcome by-product. And it seems this view is widespread. I now say, 'Thanks, but if I want exposure, I'll streak naked down O'Connell Street.' (That would mean *both* kinds of exposure. See? This is the kind of writing that shifts that sweet three units.)

Most creative people are delighted if people recognise them for good work they've done. But if all my gravestone had to say were 'She poked hornets' nests online', that'd make me really sad. Even from beyond the grave. Now I come to think about it, maybe 'She streaked naked down O'Connell Street' isn't actually the worst epitaph. Maybe I'll get on that, dropping my sponsored faux fur coat at the Parnell monument and going for it. Maybe that will take me soaring up the mysterious celebrity alphabet to N.

30

THERE'S SOMETHING ABOUT MILLENNIALS

I read great pieces every now and again on HeadStuff (and else-where) by people in their twenties sick of older generations doing them down.

I'm of that doing-down generation, so let me say this to them: *Lay off my younger buddies, alright?* I'm not even sure what you're getting from talking smack about millennials. A little rush of ex-citement to lift you out of your armchair? A heady chaser for your pub philosophy pint? Bitter exhilaration that makes you feel young, like you did when you were forty-two and could still see your toes?

There is nothing to be gained by slamming people younger than you are. They may not have experienced what you have, as many times as you've experienced it, but it's likely they've been through things as tough as – if not tougher than – you have, and they have to look great on Insta while they do it too.

I'm seeing things that aren't even generational being used as insults against them. 'Snowflakes' you call them (that again? Get a thesaurus, lads, seriously) when they're required to be tough as nails but kind on top of it, when in truth they should be giving us all a good kick in the balls. It might give us that elusive rush the naysayers seem to be chasing; the endorphins might take our minds off the fact that we're looking for a target where there really is none.

Our doing-down generation keeps looking down on millen-nials and I just can't. First of all, they're making and doing such interesting stuff that to dismiss it would make my sad old life BORING as well as growing ever more sad and old. Just like yours.

Those who are most dismissive of them are probably the type who will only listen to someone they think of as a peer. Someone who's lived as long (and fucked up as much) as themselves. As me. So, maybe take it from me? You're wrong. Back off. All you achieve by discounting people based on their youth is stagnation. You really think you've nothing to learn from them? Then pop the ol' clogs off now, 'cos you're dying where you sit. Wouldn't you rather live? (Yeah, I went there! Boom! Pow!)

We can hardly ask them not to discount us if all we have to offer is disdain. It's already tough enough for us ageing ones out there; let's not let bitterness limit us even further. Or do; you know, whatever, but see if it makes you any less bitter. Bitterness is exhausting.

This isn't about wearing clothes clearly not made with our knobbly knees in mind, or getting our sagging breasts out for the lads; it's not about trying to be Cool Teacher. Nor is it about pretending to know about memes, or how to say 'GIF', or using slang already out of date by the time we become aware of it. But it is about respect. It's about acknowledging that age is just another perspective. We may know some stuff, but we also messed up loads, and millennials are the ones now having to deal with it.

Let's cut us all some slack. Don't try too hard. But do try. They aren't aliens. They're us then, now.

Just like us, they're awash with outsiders. We all felt we were too, but now there's a culture that punishes that 'outsiderness' and rewards it with radicalisation. It siphons sadder kids off from the flock and fuels their anger, online and off, till they take their hatred out into the real world, maybe even swinging by the swastika shop. We never had to contend with all that. We were our own worst enemies. The stakes are higher now; our legacy is uncertain. It is millennials – the ones you're doing a great job of alienating – who will be working hard to understand and clean up this mess that we helped to make. Thank goodness they are clever and kind. The world is in good hands. Stop calling them snowflakes. Give them a hand. And I really think you need that thesaurus – you only seem to know three words. Aul' wans like me and you should know at least five.

Millennials: please do not catch this bitterness. It's everywhere and highly contagious. Because it is seductive: it's lovely to project what you wished for yourself and didn't get onto someone else and say they're the ones without talent, who've failed, who haven't put the work in.

Aul' wans everywhere, I hear your silent roar: IT'S NOT MY FAULT THAT TIME MARCHED ON. But it's not theirs either, friend. Taking our inadequacies out on them is a pointless waste of energy.

There will always be somebody younger, more relevant than us. Look: in the time it took to read that, there are even more. That's how it works. We can resent them and try to undermine them, or we can do our best to make sure they have an easier time; this way is, I feel, a lot more craic. This way, we learn from them. There is plenty we've learned by having lived, but they have new ways, different angles. Maybe ask them about it, sometime. They won't bite, if you don't.

31

AIR RAGE-IN

Let me start this piece by clarifying that I like other humans. I really do. I know that in a book called *Rage-In* it's possible to lose sight of that. I really do believe we all have the capacity – deep down – to be funny and clever and kind. But, Christ help me, put us in an airport and we all turn into fuckwits.

I'm not sure what it is: the lighting? The air con? Are people distracted by the presence of gift-wrapped smoked salmon? Hard to say. But grown-ups who are probably excellent parents and run major corporations and are adept at everything else in their busy lives become utterly, utterly inept as soon as they enter a departure lounge.

This doesn't include first-time fliers. They get a pass. Airports are big and baffling. It's no wonder they fill them with bars called things like 'On One Wing' or 'The Sodden Apron' or 'Aaaargh!' – air travel would drive you to drink. There is no suggestion in this piece that people come onto the planet fully and automatically equipped for flying. Even taking all that into account, there are things that happen in the airport that I'm certain these otherwise perfectly rational people just wouldn't do elsewhere. Or would they?

There's the 'Disneyland stop'-ing; forgetting there are other people at the airport, all going in several different directions, and that you might want to check your periphery before abruptly stopping with your giant backpack and set of skis to read a sign, causing a massive pile-up and taking eyes out left and right. I have done zero research on this but I can 100 per cent state as fact that these are the same complete tools who drive slowly in the fast lane, hemming everyone in. Or, worst of all, they're the people who come out of shop doorways without looking right or left, as if the pavement is theirs. It's not over-dramatic to state that they are just awful, awful people.

There are the security belt hogs. They ignore the twenty million screens on the approach to security, advising them to remove their belts and take their laptops out of their bags. They arrive with enough gear to conquer Everest, none of their liquids in 100 millilitre bottles or squished into the requisite see-through plastic bag. They will have passed seventeen see-through plastic bag dispensers on the way, written in several languages and with helpful pictures with *NO*-lines drawn through scissors, chilli powder and large fizzy drink bottles, but pesky safety measures (and don't get me wrong, some of them are fierce annoying) are clearly not meant for such as them. They probably start a fight with the guard about why they don't want to hand over their gallon bottle of cola (*they will probably have cola wherever you're going, friend*), or their homemade fireworks, or their handgun, or whatever. Either way, large backlogs will form behind them.

There are the foostherers.[1] Once you actually get on board the aircraft and take your seat and stow your hand luggage as the ladies and gentlemen of the cabin crew repeatedly tell you, there will always be three or four people foosthering and keeping the plane from taking off on time. Foosthering can take several forms: sitting in the wrong seat and insisting that they're not (and definitely not apologising, even when it escalates and has to be sorted out by an air marshal – if only we had them on trains); it can manifest

---

1   Foosthering: from the Irish fústar (to fuss or fidget pointlessly). Usually denoted 'fooster' in English. I've added an 'h' here, to make sure you all pronounce it as it should be pronounced.

as wandering up and down the aisle after the plane has started taxiing; talking on mobiles after the crew has indicated to turn them off, even though everybody knows that keeping your phone on during a flight re-routes it through the Bermuda Triangle and everyone disappears and they have to make a documentary about you all. Nobody wants to have a documentary made about them, especially one with sad/scary music, or an excuse for people that haven't disappeared to go to Bermuda to make it.

Arm-rest invaders, seat-back kickers, shoulder-droolers: these dreadful personae only reveal themselves after their seemingly-all-right alter egos have checked in. An already nervous flyer, my own trips are fraught even before I encounter them. I have to remind myself that they are good, decent people gone a bit doolally with the travel, because inside, I'm screaming: *JUST GET ON! THEN SIT DOWN! SAKE!*

I'd be more than happy to work with airlines giving seminars in this technique.

JUST GET ON, THEN SIT DOWN.

Because of my own nervousness, I approach every trip as if it's my last. That's why the foostherers upset me so much: I'm afraid I'm going to die. Every time. I'm convinced of it. And I don't want my last view to be of someone foosthering about with a bag that clearly wouldn't fit in an overhead locker if you unpacked it completely and then sawed it in half. I want my final thoughts to be compassionate, friendly ones, not 'YOU PEOPLE? I'M GOING TO DIE WITH YOU PEOPLE?'

Cabin pressure, indeed.

32

WHO HAS TIME TO BE FANCY?

I don't know how fancy people do it, but I'm in awe of them. I've never actually sat down with a calculator and worked out the hours of the day fanciness must take, but it's undoubtedly a lot. Fancy people seem to be some kind of time wizards.

I wake up really early because I have a dog who needs to be let out and a cat who walks across my face when she wants breakfast. Who needs an alarm? Peeling my pillow off the other cheek, I kiss my husband good morning, and then – unless it's Valentine's Day or some other occasion when one of us is being generous and will offer (not *that*!) – we have a short but silent stand-off regarding whose turn it is to do zoo chores. It's very democratic, very fair. No one takes the piss (except the dog, when he gets outside).

I may have a caffeinated beverage while checking the day's news and descending into a deep puddle of depression at The Shitness. Then I have another cup of caffeine and a deep breath, shelve the Ire-land and World Shitness and turn any remaining strength to my own shit. I break the day into compartments. Shit Lists help. I may not be able to do anything for Syria from here, but I can't let that stop me doing the things I can do. *Even if you can't clean the whole shithouse, start with a shitcorner.* That kind of thing.

During any given day, there will be work and meetings and worrying and admin and deadlines or no meetings and no dead-lines and therefore much more worrying. Worrying takes up a lot of hours. How on earth would you ever fit fanciness in? In between worrying, I'll take the dog for his proper walk, clean out the cat litter and we might watch a couple of episodes of *The Americans* before falling into bed much earlier than anyone has ever thought possible for two adult humans. This isn't one of the million articles about how over-worked everyone is, though. Even though we all clearly are. What it is is a related question: where do fancy people get the time to be fancy?

If reality shows have taught me anything, it's that the secret to success seems to be fanciness. There's never a blow-dried hair out of place. Nails are always so freshly manicured the lingering acetone stings your eyes through the screen and you never, ever see a ragged cuticle.

It's not just on telly, though; jaw slack on my coffee-stained parka, I see these fancy dans everywhere. If I'm walking the dog at dawn, there will already be coiffures and talons and wedges wafting through the park ahead of me. That must mean that the wafting person got up at 5 a.m. and let a team of at least three wafting specialists have at them.

God, I'd love a team.

Meet Juan, my personal trainer. He's from Spain and won't say why he moved here. Don't ask. I don't care, it doesn't matter, because he's a fitness god. While I sleep, he gently teases the cat's paws off my forehead and manipulates my limbs into long, lean perfection-stems. When I wake, I feel confused but energised and my clicky back is sorted right out.

There's Theresa, my personal chef. She's downstairs peeling and chopping for hours before I rise, making me green smoothies or exotic fruit salads which really set me up for the day so much better than batch toast with too much peanut butter. It's almost all thanks to Theresa my skin is so fabulous, but then …

… her twin sister Tanya is my dermatologist! I couldn't believe it when I got a sister-sister twin team. Tanya gives me facials

whenever my skin looks dull, which is all the time. (Dull for me, that is: obviously, thanks to the sisters, my skin is never less than regular-people radiant.) Sometimes, a facial has to happen on the go, so I get wheeled into the back of a van on a gurney and Tanya can work on my grey (for me), tired (for me), angry, lazy, petulant (the rest of you on a good day) skin while I'm on the way to another appointment. This saves a lot of time.

The person to whom I owe everything is my assistant, Barry. Barry knows where it's at. Barry knows where I'm going (and am meant to be next). Barry holds my diary – and my hand when the nerves kick in … or when we need to strategically mask a fraying cuticle.

It's thanks to Barry that I am so fancy – that I have time to get my nails done and my back massaged. To have lunches and brunches forever, where everyone wears white suits they have time to source and maintain. Pets take less maintenance than a white suit: they may not have to be dry-cleaned but, if they did, you can be sure Barry would remember to pick them up and not leave them there like that duvet from back in January.

See, now, that's me. I've done that. I do that; I forget duvets. Because Barry, sadly, isn't real. Is it any wonder my cuticles are ragged and I honestly can't imagine them being dealt with in the foreseeable future?

One day, ONE DAY GODDAMIT, I'll be at a day-long lunch with lovely nails and sleek hair and Syria will have been sorted and my deadlines met and I'll dab my exquisitely glossed lips and there will be fresh cut roses on the table because that's all that will be left requiring our attention. Not Syria, but centrepieces. Fancy that.

33

IRELAND, NOT AS ADVERTISED

Ireland, the tourism posters will tell you, is full of surprises.

Oh! The beaches! The restaurants! The pristine Aran jumpers and harps that pop up out of nowhere. The scenery that's the perfect backdrop for everything from a marriage proposal to a will-reading. The mist! The music! The smiles! The welcomes! Ohhh! Ahhh!

That's how it's sold, anyway.

The first surprise for many when they come here is that everything isn't powered by turf and we don't all have donkeys. I'd like one, as you know. (I know how to do the hitching.) Donkeys are cool. Eco-friendly too.

When the overseas guests actually arrive, however, they see that Ireland, on the surface at least, looks different from the ads. It looks like its heart: young, progressive, exciting. They come expecting to find us barefoot, only to discover many of us wear shoes. We have computers and everything. We drink lattes and share them on Snapchat. They hear that we don't all say 'turty-tree' for thirty-three, and even if we do, who the fuck do you think you are to take the piss out of us for it? (You probably shouldn't be surprised that we swear. We do.)

Other things tourists can be surprised by:

A shamrock has three leaves, not four; what you're looking at there is a four-leaf clover, a different thing entirely. The whole point of the shamrock was that St Patrick (*Paddy, not Patty*) used it to teach the Holy Trinity. Three, see? It has to be three. Or 'tree' if you're taking the piss and who the fuck … etc?

We're not thick. That's all there is to that point, really. We're not thick. We're a bit annoyed at those who've gone before us peddling us as simple, humble, thick folk.

Ireland isn't a theme park. It's a real, working country. Don't hold up traffic, pedestrian or otherwise, while you take a selfie in front of a building now owned by a bank; we have places to be. Mainly because we have to work every minute between now and our deaths to pay off that bank, or someone else who's paying off that bank. Honestly, step out of the way. This is for your own safety.

Most of those 'Mither Macree' songs you think are Irish were written in Hollywood by people who'd never been to the Mither (*what?*) Country; you won't hear them at our trad sessions, so there's no point learning them before you get here. Save yourself the bother.

But perhaps the most surprising thing about Ireland is that, just when you think things couldn't get any grimmer, they can. They always can. For a nation that loves a story, there are some we've become expert at not telling. We have looked away. We have a great, big, green carpet that we roll over anything unsavoury and we hope the lumps won't show us up. But they always do, because they never actually go anywhere.

We revere the Irish Mammy (never 'Mither'), but we spurn her, still, if she's not married. She is judged if she takes reproductive rights into her own hands, she is judged if she continues a pregnancy alone and then she is ignored, even left to the streets if it comes to it. While John Hinde was at the height of taking pictures of redheads in glorious technicolour and Bunratty was touting banquets and nearness to Shannon (and therefore, America), young women here were still being locked up. Their labour exploited. Their lives ruined. Their reputations gossiped about, torn apart in whispers. *They were lucky to have somewhere to go: the nuns were fierce good. Their souls were saved from the awful sin of sex and, sure, if a bit of washing got done or some wigs got made in return, sure what harm?* We may never know quite what harm. But it's time to take stock.

When I think of all the things I must have known, somewhere deep down, about what lay hidden in our country, I feel physically ill. I didn't *know-know* those things; they were buried deep and dark precisely so I wouldn't know-know them. But revelations, such as the infant bodies at a Tuam Mother and Baby Home, come as no surprise. It's shocking, but it's no surprise. Why is that? Because the stories that we tell ourselves to avoid the truth are the ones that Ireland's best at.

We've become experts at selling Ireland. That seems to be the main drive now, above taking care of citizens. *Shut up, put on your good coat, smarten up and tug your forelock for the paying guests. Cosy up to fascists. Whatever it takes.*

I have no doubt that St Patrick had good intentions when he 'saved' us from paganhood. But our pagan past looks pretty awesome right about now. It is a big surprise for many visitors quite how empty churches have become on this supposedly Catholic isle, and that this hasn't been brought about by protests, or campaigning – most people have no issue at all with what someone chooses to practice privately and in their own time. No, the Church's decline has been hastened along by the Church itself. The only reason it's taken so long to become this disillusioned with an institution that covered up so much harm is the fact that we all helped. I hate that I somehow helped, but I must have. The only way forward now is to accept responsibility and aim to heal.

So, tourists, lovely tourists. You are very welcome! *Fáilte*. We need you, quite frankly, and most of you are nice enough. Thanks for the money. But Ireland as advertised is no longer for sale. We're shutting up shop for a bit till we know what and who we are. And though we shouldn't be, no one's more surprised than us.

REPEAL THE INEQUALITY[1]

---

1 In this section, I take a look at various injustices and inequalities. A note: when speaking about reproductive rights, I'll refer not just to women but to 'pregnant people': transgender, non-binary and intersex people can get pregnant too. They are affected by Ireland's Eighth Amendment and often further stigmatised and discriminated against. So, in a chapter about inequality and inclusion, I'll be trying not to do that.

34

I AM THAT WITCH

It's a few years since anyone was burned at the stake in Ireland. There was that poor woman who haunts half the properties in Kilkenny, but since she went up in flames, you're not really supposed to do witch hunts any more. We're much more civilized now, even if we suspect someone has a devotion to crystals and more than one cat.

But if you ever want to rouse a baying mob, howling for your blood (and come on, who doesn't love that?) there is one last thing you can do: say the word 'abortion'. Even better, mention that you've had one. Some people won't be long dragging you to the village square for a good old-fashioned shaming. I should know. I am that witch.

Of course, instead of village squares these days we have the internet, and with it everyone's presumed entitlement to have their say or a right good old go. Thankfully, it turns out that's only a tiny part of the picture of the response since publicly sharing my own story. But I'll come back to that.

In 2015 I spoke publicly about having travelled to the Netherlands for an abortion. Abortions themselves aren't news in Ireland: even though, thanks mostly to the Eighth Amendment to the constitution, they're all but illegal here (in practice, the legal framework pretty much prohibits them completely),[1] we all know

---

1 Article 40.3.3 of the Irish constitution – inserted in 1983 and known as the Eighth Amendment – states: 'The State acknowledges the right to life of the unborn and, with due regard to the equal right to life of the mother, guarantees in its laws to respect, and, as far as practicable, by its laws to defend and vindicate that right.' This means a foetus has fully equal rights with the pregnant person

someone who's had one. It's a common procedure. Not a pleasant one – a crisis pregnancy is the furthest thing from pleasant you could imagine – but definitely common. And simple. The decision leading to it isn't straightforward, but the procedure is. Reaching that decision is one of the hardest things many people ever have to do, but once their mind is made up and they've explored every option, sometimes termination is the only way for them. If they could only access it legally and safely.

But here in Ireland, you can't. So you're forced to explore other 'options': either max out your credit card on flights and accommodation, not to mention the procedure itself, to get yourself to Britain or the Netherlands or anywhere this kind of medical care is available, or you stay in Ireland and continue a pregnancy you didn't choose and with which you cannot cope. For many, this is too much. Think the days of hurling yourself down stairs, crashing the car 'just enough', or using coat hangers are gone the way of witch-burnings? Think again. That's happening to pregnant people who can't afford to travel or whose visas don't allow them to, today. *Today*. Let me say that again, just so's we're clear: that stuff is happening today.

So I decided to tell my story, in an attempt to give a human face to the abstract numbers (roughly ten travel each day, more risk fourteen years in prison for ordering abortion pills online – that's right, it's not just illegal, it's a criminal offence) and the people demonised for making this choice.

You know what's the craic? When anonymous eejits react to your story of crisis pregnancy with such wisdom and compassion as 'Why not close your legs, slut?' or 'If you didn't want to get

carrying it. It means, as soon as you're pregnant you lose your autonomy. There is absolutely no mention of healthcare for people without wombs in the constitution. It's a highly unequal article altogether.

pregnant, shoulda used contraception, ya thick bitch!' Oh boys, THANK YOU. Why didn't I think of that? Because we all know contraception always works. You know, mostly it does. I've been sexually active for a loooong time now (I'm very old) and pregnant only once. I know about contraception, thanks for 'splainin'. Actually, on this occasion I'd taken a morning-after pill. Yes, it can happen, Judgey Judgerson. Still feeling quite so cocky?

Then there are words like 'Murderer'. 'Killer'. 'Evil'. All I can tell you is what I personally believe: it isn't murder. I couldn't have done it if that's what I believed. Many people do believe that, but many, many more do not, particularly at the very early stages of pregnancy, which is when most abortions take place. My belief still didn't make it an easy decision, but it did make it clear. This is one of the main reasons I'm pro-choice; it doesn't matter what I believe – each individual has to be free to choose what they do, according to their beliefs. It seems so obvious to me that no one should interfere in this incredibly personal decision: not the state, not concern trolls, not anyone. I hope you never are faced with it. But if you are, I hope all the options are safely available to you.

The most judgemental voices – the lads and lassies leading the shame posse, torches aflame – tend to be those who've literally never thought about what they (or someone close to them) would do in that situation. FYI, you simply can't know until you're in it. I didn't. But the statistical likelihood is that someone close to them *has* been in this situation, 'gone to England' and 'sorted it out' and never told. Some people don't even tell their mums. Ever. Especially if their surname is Judgerson.

I mentioned that shaming was only part of the picture after I went public. When I decided to tell my story and stand with the people having to travel, as well as the many more forced into horrific situations at home, I had a secret hope that times had changed. For all the *bitchwhorekillerslut*-slingers out there, or those gleefully challenging me to 'debate' the most personal aspects of my life, there was so much more love. Support. My inbox flooded with people's own stories. Finally, we know each other when we meet. We nod, 'I know.' Hundreds of thousands of us. And we're sick of being called criminals by our own country, or having our constitution declare us equal to a fertilised egg.

I have emceed the Abortion Rights Campaign's March for Choice three times now. Since 2015 it's been with full disclosure. There I stood, in the village square, warts and all. But nobody set me on fire. Not a torch in sight. Thousands more each year publicly raised their voices in support of their sisters, mothers, friends and wives. Something has shifted. Something has unstuck. The witch hunters may still be out there, but my feet? My feet haven't even been singed.

35

TWO-FACED

January is named for Janus, the two-faced god. Supposedly, he had two faces on his one head – one for looking to the future, one looking back to the past. It sounds amazing, really, and you'd probably get double your usual errands done, although I can't find much out about the logistics: did he have to walk sideways, like a crab, or what? There are no accounts of Janus bumping into stuff, so the heads must have agreed on a direction, at least. But who got the first bite of a sandwich? Who chose the sandwich? Was one of them old-school retro all the way, the other achingly progressive? How did they decide what the outfit for the day would be? And who would tie the tie?

Unlike the dreary month named after him, Janus is fascinating – though it's unlikely that he still walks the earth, sideways or not, or that he might unexpectedly drop in to your flat. Which is just as well – think of the last-minute tidying up you'd have to do, knowing you could be judged two ways at once? Luckily, as if to make up for his absence, two-faced mortals are ten-a-penny.

We're all a little bit two-faced. Come on! You know it's true. But some people seem to actively enjoy the duplicity. This kind of two-faced longs to show itself, to reveal its true colours, like a shitty peacock. It wastes a lot of energy pretending soundness but can't resist an opportunity to break cover. It thinks it's an evil – albeit sound – genius. It claims moral high ground. It's exhausting and unexpected, though you don't have to trap or trick it – it walks into traps it lays for itself. That's handy because once you have the measure of such two-facedness, you never have to deal with it again.

Trolls, for instance: they dress themselves up as online crusaders, but rarely do more in the real world than clean crumbs off their laptops. All-type-and-no-action, these are the people who hop onto an argument as if it were a battle stallion. But the stakes for them are low. They are generally chasing an adrenaline rush, spoiling for a fight and spoiling others' days. That's the pinnacle of the achievement. They want to lecture, not resolve. They want to feel great about themselves.

Like the people who say they're 'Pro Life' but don't care if that leaves pregnant people's lives at risk. Those who say 'I care about children' but never campaign for lone parents or childcare or access to education for all. The ones who say, 'I ask because I care', badgering until you have to use the Mute button *really hard*. Fat shamers, grief police, concern trolls: I hate to generalise (I love it, really. See? I'm two-faced too) but it seems that, across all issues, these inactive activists are intrusive, relentless and – it must be said – a little aroused by themselves. Irrespective of their gender I always imagine them with tiny online hard-ons.

And you know what? They're entitled to get their rocks off. I have nothing against anyone having a hobby, even a sexy one, so long as I can reach 'Mute' with my Troll Pole™. So long as they stay in an online environment.

Sometimes, though, they slither out into the real world. Like the time I was home for a family celebration, early one New Year. Over one came, all small-voiced and coy, saying how well we were looking (wait, did the lights flicker just then?), smiling thinly. Laughing at my feeble jokes – I wouldn't waste the big guns on them – but I do admit I made some (was that my own second face, revolving into position?). Their expression a sort of attempt at serenity or piety you'd arrange your own (first) face into for a funeral, say, or a long Mass, if you still went to Mass. This person definitely does. And now they're reminding you that they do, and that their faith is strong, and that that's how they know how awful you are, and steadily their second face grinds almost audibly round to the front, thin smile vanishing, soft voice setting hard, and you realise you're being ambushed. The words are polite, but the content is hostile. It's about me. My made-public personal life. This person I used to know disapproves and is determined to feel superior, and hijacking a family gathering is apparently the way to go about it. (I later discover they had already brought this faux-concern, Christian-like, to my mother's doorstep, big brave knight that they are.)

But no one is fooled. This kind of behaviour is basically like having an online wank out in the open. Without having to consult each other, my family and I engage our own second faces with rictus smiles and stony silence, and once he's said his unasked-for piece, we show the person the door. We decide there's an upside: we're actually pretty grateful to know who to cross the street to avoid from now on. Still, though, when the internet comes to life, it's a bit of a shock.

But maybe it's the month for it.

36

REPEAL

I wish I didn't have to write this but, you know, we all wish a lot of things.

Of course I'm going to write about other forms of inequality. Ireland isn't short of them and they could all do with repealing. But I'm not a politician and repeal of the Eighth Amendment is one form of inequality that I see affecting not just myself, but strangers who talk to me about their own experiences. Some of them are shocking. This is urgent. That's why I decided to speak publicly about my own crisis pregnancy and subsequent abortion. I don't regret it, though I wish I hadn't had to have one. I wish the morning-after pill had worked, but it didn't. I wish I'd felt capable of parenting. I wish I'd found being pregnant a wonderful, magical experience; instead I felt trapped by my body, then my country. I was just lucky enough to have a credit card.

I don't want anyone to go through what I did, travelling alone and frightened. That's why I demand change. I wish no one ever needed an abortion ever again. That's what I really want: no more abortions. I want only the people who want to be pregnant to be pregnant and for contraception to be 100 per cent effective, or for more people to just be plain lucky. Does that sound naïve? Right. Because it is.

You've never had a crisis pregnancy? You're lucky. I don't just mean that I envy you (I do); I mean the fact that you haven't is most likely down to sheer, dumb luck. Read that again. It could happen to you, your sister, or those friends down the pub who go very quiet when someone gets all judgemental. Yes. You most likely know someone who's had a crisis pregnancy and who, pale and silent, broke the Irish law.

What makes a pregnancy a crisis? What makes it not *unplanned* but *unwanted*? Or what's the difference between a *difficult*, much-wanted pregnancy and a tragically *inviable* one?

I can't say. Nor can you. Not until you complete your medical training (how's that going?) or until you are the one who finds yourself in a pregnancy that makes you scream so loud inside you can hear nothing else.

'I can't.'

'*You will.*'

'I don't know what I'll do if you force me to continue.'

'*We don't care.*'

In my case, I did my research. Talked it over and over with (just two) friends – one of whom was distraught. 'You'd be such a great mum.' I wouldn't. I knew. Only I could know. And once I was sure, I booked the clinic and flight.

I have a massive problem with the phrase 'abortion on demand'. Although, yes, we should be able to request a medical procedure when we need it. 'Abortion on demand', as used by those opposed to reproductive rights, is an attempt to erase nuance. To diminish the pain of a terrible time, the trauma of wrestling back and forth till you can say, 'Yes, I am sure.' Or at least, 'I am as sure as I can be given the best information I can get.' It's an attempt to dismiss not being able to sleep, or eat – for one, let alone two. To discount the loneliness and isolation. The terror of the pregnancy itself. That though a particular choice might be clear, it doesn't mean it's easy. 'Abortion on demand' is a phrase used to suggest that stupid women will opt for an expensive, uncomfortable procedure over readily available contraception and flippantly skip off for abortions on our lunchbreaks.

STOP. Please, stop.

In July 2016, about a year after I'd gone public, someone posted on my Facebook page, to make sure I'd see it, congratulations for 'all I was doing for abortion on demand'. The phrasing let me instantly know something was amiss, so I followed the link. There was a newly set up page featuring pictures of some of us taken for the Repeal Project – Anna Cosgrave's initiative to destigmatise repeal campaigning and make support more visible. This was largely achieved by the means of black sweaters with the word 'Repeal' printed on them in white. They not only became the must-have jumper of the time, but offered people strength and solidarity. Even if words were never exchanged between you. Someone wearing one of these jumpers was unlikely to judge or shame. On this fake (now removed) page, the word 'Repeal' across our chests had been altered. (The irony of the use of our very bodies to convey an anti-autonomy message was not lost.) My own image had been badly photoshopped to read 'Aborted my only child.'

Someone clueless about my life had tried to rob my decision of humanity. To make that decision stark and cold. To twist 'I don't regret' and 'I was relieved' into some kind of murderous boast. To trigger my memories of a difficult moment. To make my sharing of the experience a smear against me.

But they cannot. My conscience is clear. They believe in personhood from conception; I do not. They are incapable of walking a mile in anyone else's shoes. For that, I feel truly sorry for them.

To those who cried, 'Isn't it technically true?': if you think the misappropriation of images of women with the intent to smear is okay, I don't have the time to begin to explain it to you. Scratch that. I don't think you're worth explaining it to. But I'm sure you're not like that.

And to those who alleged we altered the images ourselves to

win public opinion *(#agentprovocateur!)*, you make me sick. Although a lot of public opinion was with us. Well done.

There are constant cries for 'respectful debate', but I have sat in more than one room with people sharing their stories, where someone felt morally superior enough to try to stigmatise anyone who had been unable to continue pregnancy. To trot out long-debunked myths. That is not respectful. This same perceived superiority later called for pressure to be applied to remove a pro-choice artwork from a theatre wall. We only ever seem to hear about hotels cancelling anti-choice campaign meetings, but it's happening to pro-choice groups too. This selective view of events seems to stem from the same superiority that reduces real pregnant people and our lives to collateral damage.

We now call for respect. We don't have time for distraction, myth and stigma. If you can't care enough to hear another person's lived experience and not judge, you really aren't in a position to take part in an open discussion. If you'd have done differently, that's fine. The status quo already supports you. It doesn't make you right. It doesn't give you the right to silence or shame.

You know what I see when you deny pregnant people's real, nuanced experiences? When scare tactics are not denounced? When you target an individual for telling her story? I see cruelty. Coldness. A monster. Exactly how you might describe me. And I know you don't want to be like me.

37

BOOBS OUT FOR SUMMER

Intermission –

I promised I'd take a look at other inequalities and here's a very serious one: boobs. It's time to call for equal treatment of the be-knockered.

I'm what they call 'well endowed' – as if someone was handing out boobs and I was at the front of the Queue of Endowment, claw-like hands wide open, grasping, eager. *Oh, thank you, lord of boob dispensing! What boob boon is this! Endow me! Endow me well!* But big boobs aren't as much fun as saucy postcards and *Carry On* films and Benny Hill have led some of you to believe. The kind of bouncy comedic expectations they set up, big boob owners spend a lot of time trying to deflate.

Actually, everyone thinks they're big boob owners. I don't mean they all have large breasts, but many seem to feel they have some kind of ownership over all of them. I guess they do stick out into public space a bit, but for all their faults, let me tell you: mine are nobody's but mine.

And big boobs do have faults. Jogging is sore. Backhands are tricky (another reason to ditch tennis), certain yoga postures impossible without self-strangulation. It's hard to dress big boobs; they move around and try to effect their escape. They're the closest I've come to dealing daily with unruly toddlers. 'Come back!' I say, tutting and shaking my head as they head into town without me. 'You guys!'

I'm not even that big – I'm not one of the sizes they store insensitively far from the 'regular' (what's that?) ones in lingerie departments – but I do have breasts more in-your-face than

I'd like, bigger than is strictly approved of – unless by 'approval' you mean the odd preconditioned 'phwoar'. If I don't cinch in at the waist, people assume I'm pregnant, or guide me towards the muumuus (which are a great look, if that's your natural style. It's just not mine). Being top-heavy and wearing a loose shirt means being offered seats on the bus. I take the seats, don't get me wrong; I'm no fool. But clothes are the least of it. You'd be amazed the licence breasts seem to give others to be arses.

Cat calls, wolf whistles, a whole farmyard of 'oi oi!' just for existing on a street. An assumption that you're up for it, that you carry an inflatable beach ball in your bag, ready for finger-in-the-mouth, one-leg-kicked-up poses. You are rarely described as graceful, neat. As an actor you might not get offered serious parts because … well … what if everyone sees you and assumes it's a *Porky's* reboot?

Even those who are supposed to be helping aren't helping. Bra fitters are terrifying. 'What size do you think you are?' Followed by, 'NO!' if you're wrong and then you're frogmarched away for fifteen years' hard labour (and the built-in support in the gulag jumpsuits is not meant to be up to much, so make sure and grab a bra before they drag you away).

Sometimes you wear a low-cut top because:

a) it's too hot for a polo neck/full nun's habit or

b) you liked the top on the hanger and momentarily forgot about boob etiquette,[1] or

c) because you like your boobs, goddamit, and you don't see why they shouldn't get out for a bit of air once in a while.

---

1   Boob etiquette: you are responsible for hiding your boobs OR accepting the consequences: any and all commentary, nudges and drunken, uninvited fondling. Cover those puppies up! Nothing too tight, though.

But if you do, you won't be allowed to forget that boobs are HILARIOUS. Apparently. Nobody outright laughs at my legs, or grabs at them and makes honking noises, but my breasts have got that for years. You'd think they'd be used to it. No, the shame and rage aren't lost on them yet. Ever wanted to test whether women are objects? Have prominent boobs! Once, a guy asked if he could leave his pint on my 'shelf'. And he was trying to get off with me. At least his pal had the decency to look embarrassed and take him home. Needless to say, I wanted guy number one bad. There is nothing hotter than being compared to storage: to be not even as good or interesting as a pint, but somewhere to leave it.

I enquired about reduction surgery, years ago. Tired of being a hilarious shelf, I wanted someone to carve me up and make me into a real girl, not a *Carry On* prop. I chickened out. Or rather, I got a sudden burst of bravery: I wasn't going to get cut to make somebody else's cut. And there were other factors: my morbid fear of anaesthetic, and the fact that I couldn't afford it, not to mind the idea that people were having life-saving operations while mine would only be about avoiding humiliation. It didn't sit right with me. Someday – God forbid – I might need breast surgery for medical reasons. I couldn't reconcile performing it on healthy tissue. Removing my own flesh because of taunts? Surely I could tough it out and grow to accept my hilarious roundness. Cosmetic surgery may be what you feel you need and fair play if so. I hope it makes you feel as good as you deserve to.

All I'm saying is a couple of weeks ago someone hung a walking stick in my cleavage and winked. We're married now.[2]

---

2   I left him in a skip.

38

CAN ANYBODY SEE ME?

Dear reader,

You don't vanish all at once. The erasure happens bit by bit. You fade gradually, a little each day.

'It will never happen to me,' you think, and then suddenly you're just a voice. A faint one.

The one discrimination that will happen to us all, if we are lucky enough to live that long, is ageism.

You might get through life and be lucky enough never to experience sexism, racism, transphobia or homophobia, but once you pass fifty, you are *old*. Unfresh. Unexciting. Bread you wouldn't eat. Eggs you'd throw out.

I'm going to share something shocking with you. I'm nearly fifty. Well, I'll be fifty in a couple of years – not nearly fifty at all if you're five and counting every day until you're six. But otherwise, I'm as good as fifty. In fact, in relation to twenty-five, when everything happens, I'm sixty. Or dead. But definitely starting to become invisible.

Saying, 'You look all right *for your age*' is nice to hear, but actually it's part of it. It means 'You're beating the system somehow, but not for long, Granny. And now that I know your actual age I will subconsciously start to discount you.'

MILF

Mother I'd like to fuck.

An older woman you'd *still* like to fuck! Or is it just mothers? Is it the maternity part that's attractive? Would you still fuck me, even though I've never given birth? If so, what's the acronym for that?

Cougar

Not real women. Wild beasts. Should have stopped being sexual around the normal time, say, twenty-six-and-a-half.

If you don't take care of grey hairs or wrinkles immediately you've 'given up'. When relaxing into who you really are is 'giving up', you know society has a problem with ageing. Let me tell you, fifty happens real fast. Fifty comes around in the time between an in-breath and exhalation.

I feel the same now as I did when I was twenty-five. The mirror may not match this feeling, but I have almost the same amount of energy, the same dreams. Except I'm not supposed to ask for those dreams any more. I'm supposed to fade into the background. 'You missed your go', that's how it's seen. 'If I haven't heard of you by fifty or you're not a millionaire home-owning CEO or something, well, we just don't know where to put you.'

Old women are only allowed to be wise. Feared. *Or* they can be doddery and adorable. But once fertility is gone, what real use are they? Men suffer ageism too, don't worry about that lads, but you become distinguished wizards. Whereas we might be useful for asking for an ol' recipe.

Be vigilant for the lazy trope of the hilarious old woman. Not saying we're not witty: we are. But, for example, skateboarding isn't hilarious; yet if a granny (or a stuntman dressed as one) does it, it's a laugh riot. Rapping isn't hilarious – *but haha! Look! – a woman in her seventies has heard of hip hop!* And sex? Even the most inclusive comedians use older women as punchlines. 'And who was giving me the blow job? Her mother!' Our foremothers *invented* blow jobs and unusual positions because it was cold outside and there was no telly. I don't want to make you think about your own nan inappropriately, I'm just saying *don't write Nana's skills off.*

Post-menopause, women aren't supposed to be physical beings any more, so we erase them from popular culture.

The women in the ads are all eighteen or Helen Mirren, who we love, but she has genes and money with which most of us cannot compete. I don't see a representation of myself on-screen, not enough. And if you live long enough, all of this will happen to you.

Older men are sometimes rewarded, while women pay for surviving the rest of the shit. The years don't make us 'tough', they make us 'worn'.

Not giving a fuck

The best bit about getting older is the not giving a fuck. *Granny DGAF.* But it isn't as simple as that. You do give fewer actual fucks but once you're invisible it's the only way to get things done. The social contracts you use when you're young abandon you. If you make eye contact with a bartender or server now, it's 'creepy' in a way it never was before. No longer just a bit of fun while you wait for your sandwich or beer. Not a silly social way to make sure they remember you. Those little daily interactions go. They don't see you. No wonder you'll stand up, after forty minutes, on a stool, twirling your handbag over your head crying, 'For Gods' sake, sonny, gimme my fucking wine!'

You do fade physically. You have to do a lot of squats and lunges to make sure things don't lose density and break, down the line. You see things happen again and again, fashions coming in and out. But do you get credit for it? No. And proper order: you shouldn't get extra respect just because you got here first. But nor should you get less because you'll be gone first too.

You don't lose your vitality, your self. I'm still in here, hearing all the reasons why such unfreshness shouldn't be on TV or – before I met my husband – *why I'm still single at my age: what was wrong with me?* Age as a reason to dump you. To not date you in the first place.

We see the documentaries, undercover in care homes, showing how – though most carers are wonderful – sometimes even those who are paid to care, do not. Would that attitude be so prevalent if wider society didn't rush to bury older people before they are dead?

I'm not saying 'Visit your nana more!' She might be an awful human. Instead, question why you don't see her in magazines or on-screen. Until we see it we can't change it. I'm just asking you to see it.

If a movie has a lazy granny-having-sex scene, instead of saying, 'Ew, granny sex ha ha!', go 'Wow, looks like Chad will have learnt some new moves. Lucky Chad.' Laugh with us. Not at us. Maybe we'll be having so much fun together there'll be more inter-generational interaction and people won't throw you on the scrap heap either when your time comes.

For now, I fight the heap with all my might.

It. Will. Happen. To. You.

It's in the post. So let's change things. For your granny now, and for your skateboarding, rapping, no-limits self to come.

Yours sincerely,

a tiny disembodied voice.

REPEALING THE INSCRIPTION: AN ISLAND'S PLEA FOR EQUALITY

In recent times in Ireland – finally! – we've been hearing a lot about abortion rights and the need to repeal the Eighth Amendment, as well as lots of arguments against this notion (most ideology-based and with plenty of misdirection, but that's another story). I, for one, won't be voting in any general elections, forever, for anyone who doesn't have a strong stance on letting the people have their say, at the very least.

In a bid to make themselves seem both progressive and well, *not*, politicians had (at least up until the findings of the Citizens Assembly and Joint Oireachtas Committee in 2017 where findings leaned far more towards a pro-choice stance and broad access than many predicted) been attempting a splits-like straddling move, not unlike Jean Claude Van Damme in that ad with the two trucks. They would consider access to abortion in Ireland, but only in exceptional cases. To be fair, these are the hard cases that, shockingly, haven't been dealt with till now: cases of rape, incest or fatal foetal anomaly. Heartbreaking cases. Obvious, clear crises.

But that didn't deal with the rest of us. The unexceptional. The majority. Those who, like me, faced a crisis perhaps not so clear-cut to others, but a crisis nonetheless. Are we to continue to be ignored – ten or so of us a day condemned as criminals and forced to travel? It may ease certain consciences – they may even see it as a 'gentle' way to broach the issues of bodily autonomy and reproductive rights – but the truth is that such an approach would change little.

In fact, it's quite brutal. It would leave most of us stranded. And guess what? We are voters too.

I was angrily thinking about this last week, while walking on a fictitious beach. To my surprise, I found a fictitious bottle bobbing on the shoreline. There was a fictitious letter in it, voicing a very real cry for help:

I am marooned on an island. It's not paradise, although coconuts have recently become plentiful. Not all year round, don't be ridiculous. They are still expensive and prized. But you can get their milk in a can almost anywhere and their water comes in a carton as a status symbol, for some reason.

I am not alone. We are many. For the most part, island life is all right. Many of us have shelter and, if you believe all the tourism ads, the craic is only ninety. In the ads, we eat lobster and windsurf all day long – often at the same time. In the ads, we have no problems.

The island is mysterious, but unlike the cast of Lost, *we didn't crash here and we can leave any time we like. In fact, leaving is encouraged. That's part of the problem. (Ironic, as we supposedly don't have any. Problems, that is. You've seen the posters!) We handle these not-problems our own way. We'll tackle excessive social drinking by putting up the price of alcohol (wine is already the price of a small car, or three coconuts). We'll tackle unemployment figures by getting people on 'internships' forever for zero coconuts. And unwanted pregnancies ... Well, there are none.*

For we are fortunate to be situated right beside The Island of Solution. It was decreed that any not-problems be sorted there, in silence. IT IS WRITTEN, and so it shall be. You shall not contradict the windsurfing ads.

Three long decades ago, our fates were sealed by elders you don't hear much of nowadays. We assume they wandered over to the other side of the island like half of the cast of Lost. *They believed in magic, so perhaps it's apt that they have vanished. But, carved onto a big stone, their will remains. You couldn't really fault the stone itself. It's a fine stone. But it stonily states that half of us are not equal and that verily must we take ourselves across the sea to 'sort things out, on the down-low, if you know what I mean'. This is followed by a symbol, worn with age, which archaeologists believe to be a winky face.*

You would think that the remaining elders would be happy with those who comply and leave the island. But they don't want to know. Almost as if half of us were worth nothing – definitely much less than a coconut. Even an off-season coconut. The idea of being fruitful, like a great big palm tree, is of value. The fruit delivery system or 'woman', less so.

Non-islanders may find this hard to understand but these are our ways. We don't get it, either, but it's on the fecking stone.

Elders make sad faces but these faces are fake. All unwilling fruit delivery systems, regardless of circumstance, are forced into escape canoes and then condemned for getting into them. While the stone still stands, we must keep the escape canoes bobbing in the secret cove and hope we have enough coconuts for passage.

On this island, being fruitful is the law. And you can cope. You can. You've read the stone. Carved in small print at the bottom, worn from much touching, is a reminder: 'Plenty more where you come from, girl.'

We are weary of being sent away, deserted. The elders may have ears for the urgent cases; what about the rest of us? The beaches are overflowing. There are not enough canoes.

We dream of a day we will not be forced to leave the island. So we are sending out these messages and smoke signals in the hope they'll be seen from the air. In the sand we've spelled out 'Help us'.

Perhaps that help will never arrive. But even if it doesn't, know this: we're worth more than a fucking coconut.

40

BUTT OF THE JOKE

Boom! Another explosion, right in your unexpectant face. It's so hard to navigate the world these days, now that it's literally a minefield. *Literally*. Except that, of course, these aren't literal mines and the fields aren't real. But it doesn't matter – the effect is *exactly the same*. You're walking along the street, or posting on your favourite forum, doing and saying whatever you want without consequence, when someone comes up and asks you *not* to say something, which is exactly the same as punching you right in the nose FOR NO REASON. It's a wonder you don't just walk out of your house with just a few shirts and some sandwiches in your backpack, never to return. Leave the door open, it doesn't matter. This is a war zone. Let the marauders have your stuff.

Now, I would watch that movie. In fact, I do watch that movie. It's on every day, wherever you come across other people, on or off-line. There is high drama attached to causing or experiencing what some reduce to 'offence'. Drama which, if you manage to stay off to the side, might almost be entertaining if it weren't so tiresome. 'Political correctness gone mad' has become a redundant phrase. It seems the mere existence of political correctness itself, not going anything like mad, is cause enough for affront. Political correctness at home on a Saturday night, watching *The Ray D'Arcy Show* with a cup of cocoa and its fluffiest socks on, that's enough to tip people over the edge into talk of mines and explosions and curtailing of freedoms.

'How do we know what's right or wrong any more?' people wail. Well, is the thing you're saying something you would say in front of the people it's about? And still allow them to have a fun day? Because that's really all there is to it. This isn't about groups or individuals being sense-of-humour deficient; it's the difference between being slagged while in on the joke, or being the butt of it. It's no fun being a butt. Literally.

I was the only woman backstage at a comedy club once. A comic I'd never met before made a joke about my cleavage and how it looked like a butt. Everyone laughed. It was funny. So why did I feel like crap? It's nice to be useful. An accessory. Yet again, a prop. But that's what I was reduced to. I was required only to stand there, me and my butt-chest, like an unwilling magician's assistant, handing out butt-chests when needed. I felt uncomfortable, so I said so; myself and this lad had it out and ultimately ended up friends. It might have been a small bit risky, but I had no option but to say something: I was worn out after years of *teehee, boobies!* jokes and I turned into a bit of a landmine myself.

As Caitlin Moran wrote, sometimes, when someone is what the landmine-merchants call 'touchy', it's really because they're tired. What's a throwaway one-off to you might be something they live with all the time. Maybe they even laughed at their own breasts the first time; weakly, so as not to rock the boat. The fiftieth time, their last nerve frayed, they'd happily sink the boat to get off it.

On the other side of the offence-fence, swarms or piling on are equally tiresome. In the playground or online. Divisive spats tend to go nowhere, so … maybe don't have them? No one's really listening. I wish they were; I've learned my lesson via torn-out clumps of my own hair. If you care about an issue, campaign on it. But heated back-and-forths (the kind they seem to favour on so-called TV 'debates') are as productive as shouting down a sink.

There are loads of things which, on paper, might seem to curtail or limit, but they're actually just not-bollocky things to do. Say, taking a crap on O'Connell Street. You may want to, you may even feel you urgently need to, but not doing so is going to make your day and everyone else's so much better. Trust me.

And they're not really landmines, are they? It's just substituting new words for old, less useful ones. When someone says 'I don't like it when you say X' or 'You may not realise, but it hurts when you use the term Y', why not not say X or Y any more? Of course, you're free to. But you're smart. And you're not a big shit (on O'Connell Street or anywhere else). Our heads are super-full, I get it, but we definitely still have room for a few new ideas and terms. Just because we didn't realise before doesn't mean we have to take to a soapbox with a loud-hailer and overcompensate as soon as something's pointed out. It's okay to not know, till you know. Then you know.

If you still think there are literal landmines in modern interactions, there are also plenty of signs for how to avoid them. But if you're the kind of maverick who thinks signs are only there to slow you down, well … boom.

41

A MATTER OF PRIVILEGE

I'm tired. I'm so tired. Not physically tired, although the exhaustion tendrils creep around my body sometimes too. This means I'm in less than perfect health. I'm sick. I'm sick and tired of your bullshit. Yes, yours and mine too. We are all so full of shit.

It seems it's far more important these days to work really, really hard to defend our positions, than to open our ears to learn something new, or unlearn something old and no longer useful. The previous piece, 'Butt of the Joke', is a softer version of this, a kind of phase one. But funny doesn't seem to be working. I wasn't clear enough. So now that I'm angry – yes, at you and at me too – let me be clear. Let me break this down for us.

Some of us are born with all the sweeties. What did we do to earn these sweeties? Nothing! Not a damn thing. They were just our sweeties from birth, just to have, just 'cos. And as we grow, we learn that other people don't have as many sweeties – or even any sweeties at all – and then we have a choice: to tilt our heads and go 'Aw, that's sad. But that's just how life goes,' while shovelling sweets into our mouths, so many that they block up our ears from the inside and we don't have to listen. To pop After Eights on our eyes so we can pretend not to see. To acknowledge, intellectually, that we have certain privilege points, while choosing not to enjoy them responsibly, like alcohol. Or – OR – we can choose to share the sweets we did nothing to get. We can be accountable.

I visualise my own privilege as a kind of veil: I have been barely aware of it but, whenever it lifts another little bit, a little bit more reality is visible and what's seen can't be unseen. I wasn't aware the veil was there – it was so comfortable and familiar I barely noticed it – but I didn't ask for it to be lifted, either, so I'm complicit. It doesn't matter that *I didn't mean any harm*, there's no need for me to say that, because now's my chance to learn. But if I recoil in defence, nothing changes. So, right now, I'm disappointed. I'm depressed. I'm tired of people either avoiding the truth or shouting from atop a lot of sweetie piles about 'free speech'.

I call bullshit.

Many of you know that my husband, Carl, is African-American. That's right, a black fella. I made a satirical video about abuse that he got. It's called *Racist B&B* (N.B. not a real B&B) and it can be viewed on YouTube. Now, I studied linguistics before running away to join the actors and, in the past, I have definitely taken part in theoretical discussions about using certain words to take away their power. But where the N-word is concerned, this is a luxury. This is privilege. I have never been (nor never will I be) referred to by this most vile and oppressive of terms. It is not my word. To have seen its effects on my husband's face, in his shaking hands, the to-the-core hurt it engenders chilled me to the bone. No, white people: we can't use it. Or rather, of course we can – we can do what we want, sweetie-folks – but why on earth would we want to?

You are racist. I am. As the hilarious *Avenue Q* song goes, '*everyone's a little bit racist sometimes/doesn't mean we go around committing hate crimes*'. Here in Ireland, how can we not be? When I was growing up, there were Black Babies charity boxes in every classroom. That's what they were called. The N-word was dropped right and left: even in the playground, 'Eenie Meenie Miney Mo' still had it right in there, right before 'You. Are. It'. Before I knew better, I sang along with the word in songs, used it in reported speech. I feel deeply ashamed of it now, but I am working hard to make amends and do better.

We are all a little bit sexist too. Classist. Ableist. Ageist. And so on. The bit of homophobia we all share was beautifully called out by Panti Bliss in her now globally famous noble call, delivered at the Abbey Theatre in 2014. All of the above 'isms' or 'obias' have one thing in common: they're so deeply ingrained they can feel 'normal'. But that doesn't mean we have to accept them.

White people choosing not to say or write n****r is not 'wussing out' or 'immature'. Rather it is a stance that says, 'I've heard what you said. I am listening.' Even if, as I do, you believe we are all equal, it's vital to acknowledge that we are not all treated equally. You, with the dolly mixtures clinging to the soles of your shoes, wine gums as far as the eye can see, are a lot less likely to find a reservation you made over the phone evaporate into a mysterious 'double-booking' upon your arrival, or to be incarcerated, or shot in the back for no reason.

But if you want to keep the sweeties in your ears, there's not a damn thing anyone can do to stop you. And that, right there, is privilege.

42

YOU JUST MIGHT BE
THE BAD GUYS

Remember when the pesky UN suggested – *again* – that it was time to cop ourselves on and look after pregnant people here in Ireland (among other areas in which we're failing the human rights test miserably)? Well, as you can probably tell, I've spent quite a bit of time thinking about that. Their assertion that we weren't human rights compliant made certain elements very cross ('Rubbish. Just look at the *tourism posters!*'), and they weren't long in voicing their thoughts. Everyone's entitled to their opinion. It's why pieces like this exist so, you know, great. But opinion is just that: what you think.

However, those who oppose our right to autonomy are repeatedly allowed to present opinion as fact. Time and again they are given national media platforms, unchallenged, despite having no expertise or lived experience in the matter. With soft voices, brows are furrowed and facts manipulated. The word 'sincere' is said a lot. I put this to these campaigners: perhaps you are sincere. I sometimes think you might be. But I need you to think about something.

How do I put it? It's awkward but here goes: You just might be the bad guys.

Bear with me. Your intentions may well come from what once seemed like a good place. But when you take fact – not opinion – into account, you just might be the bad guys. It's not good to be willing to say or do anything – even if it's not true – to win, when these are your potential prizes:

To have a struggling family lose their home, or go hungry when one more mouth to feed will be too many. Where will you be when they're out on the street? Not on the street, that's for sure.

Forcing an asylum seeker to birth a rapist's baby.

You would let someone die for your beliefs, not theirs.

You would let a woman carry her beloved dead within her, though she begs you to let her grieve her way.

You would meddle in a body not your own. Force a terrified person to continue with a pregnancy, when their terror comes from the pregnancy itself.

Let us travel for a procedure made more dangerous by the travelling. Have us go alone, return to shame.

Keep the dead 'alive' and tear a family's heart out for a law.

Let someone kill themselves, if they feel that's the choice.

Jail a teenager for saying she's not ready. She is wise.

Tie our doctors' hands, making them unable to administer correct care.

Congratulations. You have your prize already.

I'm certain that this is not the self-portrait you set out to paint. I'm sorry that the light's not flattering.

I had an abortion and it saved my life. But I am not an expert. Not in abortion, not in law, or medicine, and certainly not in what is right for someone else. I only tell my own story. Yet these campaigners claim expertise, authority. From whom?

Though I'm not an expert, some things are sure:

One ideology cannot be imposed on others who don't share it.

If you are opposed to abortion, no one will make you have one. Stop saying that they will.

A foetus with a fatal anomaly is not a 'disabled child'. You know that too.

Contraception does not always work. People make mistakes. The options cannot be to abstain, give birth or die.

This is not a debate. Consensus on belief is impossible, so debate is futile. Theorising 'against' someone who's faced real life trauma and given up their privacy so others might not face the same is hardly 'balance'. But if you must frame it as debate, untruth must be challenged whenever it's heard.

Study after study shows that banning abortion doesn't stop it happening. As if, in Ireland, we needed a study to tell us that.

At least ten women will travel today. Others will buy illegal pills. Others will harm themselves in desperation.

The reaction from certain quarters to the UN's statement and the ongoing campaign has been vicious but predictable. Such vitriol, I'm told, is an inevitable part of speaking out on this topic.

I'm not part of an organisation. I'm not a politician. But since speaking out a small but vocal bunch of commentators has verbally torn apart my character, how I look, my integrity, and even questioned whether or not I'm any good at my job. (I'm not.) They badger me for answers not mine to give. They call me 'Abortionist', 'Murderer', 'Slut', 'Pro abort', reduce me to just one of 'the pro-choice "crowd"'.

By that do you mean women in crisis? Grieving families? Compassionate people, even those morally opposed to abortion, who feel meddling in others' bodies and what's best for them is not right? Well, that's a crowd I'm proud to be in. A crowd that's growing by the day.

If all you have is misdirection, a distaste for human rights and slinging mud at individuals then I'm sorry – and this, of course, is just my opinion – but you just might be the bad guys. And maybe you won't win.

43

THE GHOSTS AT THE DEPARTURE GATES

A queue inches slowly towards security, foot by shuffling foot. The people in it are fluorescent-lit and cranky. Some hold holiday hats in their hands. Where will they stow them? Will they be squashed – ironically, for hats – in overhead compartments? Others impatiently check watches and fold raincoats over their arms. They have somewhere to be. In an hour. They don't have time for this. Who does?

No one, right now, is happy. *Take off your shoes, put them in a plastic box. Yes, the belt too, please. Show me your tiny toiletries? Thanks.* Frequent flyers tut. They don't have time for this. With flamboyant testiness, they zip up laptop bags with one hand, lace shoes with the other and disappear towards their gate.

I'm back at the airport.

Less expert than the frequent flying execs but certainly no slouch, I pull my boots on and slide the plastic boxes back. Just like I was taught. Good Catholic girl; leave the place better than you found it.

A flashback crackles through fluorescent. I try to blink it back. It won't blink back. Ten years. Can it be ten years? And I'm back at the airport.

The place of 'Welcome Home!' Destination and potential. *Come back soon, we'll miss you!*

You didn't miss me, then. You couldn't get rid of me fast enough.

The memory angers me. I fight, but it insists: it seems, regardless of time passing, every journey will remind me of that one. Just as shops called *Irish Memories* insist *you will be back – but take a Guinness T-shirt, just in case*! A decade ago. Alone. Exhausted. Terrified. Looking no different from the others in the queue, if a tiny bit more adept at plastic box replacement. For me, no adrenaline-fuelled executive London lunch. No morning-drinking en route to a schoolfriend's hen. For me, silence. I needed an abortion and a plane would take me to it. A journey to end a journey I did not choose to take. I closed my eyes that day and tried to taste the relief to come. It did. But not here.

Every shop sells sunglasses in this sunless, airless box of traffic. Dark lenses you can hide behind, if hiding's what you want. But I don't need them now. I'm already hidden in plain sight. That journey made me invisible.

And more than that, like someone suddenly endowed with superpowers, I see them now. *Them*. The others, just like me, have been revealed to me. Impossible to say what gives them away – nothing they say or do, I just know. Something in their eyes. Something in our shared heavy hearts. We blur around the edges just a bit, almost blending in, but not. We are beyond the rest now, set apart and silenced. Exiled on this day; stigmatised forever. We recognise the others who must make this journey, those who must find compassion away from home. But we must never say. We are the ghosts at the departure gates. Some say we don't exist. We know we do.

The men who govern use this airport too, and sometimes roll red carpets out for other men who don't deserve it. And we laugh and clap and roll our eyes. 'Ireland!' we say, while working to convince American relatives to remember the tourism posters and come and visit Cashel, like we're told to. 'Come in, come in!' we say, bowing till our noses touch the ground. We send singing women around the world, immaculate in ballgowns, debutantes, immaculate of heart and incorrupt of body. This is the ideal. This is who we Irish women should be. Red-haired, windswept, pure. That's who's on the postcards. It's not who you see being forced to leave.

The men who govern don't have private planes. They pass through here just like the rest of us, they must. And we are at their elbows, if they chose to see. They don't. They pass right through us, like the ghosts we are. On our secret missions, attachés taking the fall, ambassadors for a truth they want concealed. They look us in the eye and turn away. Every day. Every port. It is impossible our paths have not crossed. The next time you leave this island, Taoiseach, Minister, remember this. We're only feet away. And you, you are the handler: you put us on that plane. Or boat. Or worse.

Ten years ago, a flight made me feel safer than I had while on the ground. Out of Ireland. Safe. Ten years. You have not budged. But I will not forget, nor do I want to. I have been here before. I will always be here. My ghost is at the gate.

Next time you pass this way, make sure to take a souvenir. Something to remember. You must remember. And you must see it all.

44

RIDING FOR IRELAND

Intermission –
  Let me give you a little boost (I feel like you might need one).

Ireland is sexy. Hey! No sniggering, please. I'm serious. I mean it. Listen.

When I was still doing stand-up, I used to do material about how Irish people weren't sexy, about how when we took our clothes off it was less like tantalisingly revealing the beautiful gift of your naked body … more like unwrapping uncooked chicken. Our awkwardness in getting it on was more to do with fear of salmonella than anything else.

But we all know that's not true. We all know what I was skirting around there. I mean, the joke got laughs because we acknowledge the idea that our traditionally pasty skin was the problem, but it's really not true. And not just because Irish people come in all shades and colours. No, it's repression and fear and shame that got in the way of us taking the global stage as the hot pieces of ass we are. Well, those days, my lady and gentleman and non-binary friends, are over. We're taking sexy back and there's not a damn thing they can do about it.

Who are *they*? *They* are de Valera, Archbishop John Charles McQuaid and any of their frigid minions who tried to beat the sex out of us. Even enshrining a good dollop of the ol' shame in the constitution. They took what looked (even to untrained, angry eyes) like their own repressed kinks and destructive hunger for power, things a few quick therapy sessions could have ironed out and, instead, (ironically) fucked a nation for years with their warped ideas of virtue. The misery of it, the sheer, unrelenting misery. It sapped our strength. It made us compliant for far too long.

I now advocate the Riding Rebellion. It'll be like 1916, but ridier. All you have to do is have sex and not be ashamed of it. *For Ireland.* They hate it when you're not ashamed. It shouldn't be any of their business, and I'm not sure exactly who 'they' are now, but they still hate it. Let's resolve to do it more.

How dare anyone say Irish people weren't sexy or good at sex when, if they'd let it into the Olympics, we'd have won at it? I'm certain that part of the reason we didn't do well at other sporting events was we were so tired from riding and covering it up; the covering it up part being the part that took up all the time and energy.

Name a place in this country – go on, anywhere: sex has been had there. Just ask Nana. Irish people had to be inventive with where they had the sex so it looked like the sex wasn't being had. Ditches, cupboards, unlit laneways, canal banks, glassy chrome Celtic Tiger offices, cow byres, confession booths … you name it. And you know it. I'm not inventing this or revealing anything you don't know to be true. Leinster House? I wouldn't run a black-light in there. Sure, they're even glauming each other (whether the glaumee likes it or not *hahagoodgirlyourself, you'reagreatsport*) when the Dáil is in session. God knows what happens at less populated times. Alan Shatter even wrote a fiction book about it, so it's definitely true. As if we couldn't have guessed by the heads on them. And I do mean heads.

When you build shame into the constitution itself, when you remove people's responsibility to weigh their own morals and ethics and butt out of everyone else's lives, sexy or otherwise, you create a big old mess. A mess you don't need a blacklight to pick up. It's about time we took being tethered to the kitchen out of the constitution and repealed all the repression once and for all.

There's a video still knocking about online of Annie Murphy, who gave birth to the son of the late Bishop Eamonn Casey. It's of her appearance on *The Late Late Show*, during which she was openly vilified and scorned. There is glee on the faces of the audience. They are sanctimonious, self-righteous, cruel in their attempts to discredit her, when the facts of her story were undisputed. That was 1993. Another Olympic omission at which we'd excel: Curtain Twitching.

How dare we? How dare we?

It's high time to leave the curtains in the past, where they belong, and get back to what we're good at: riding. (Just ask Nana.) It doesn't matter that it's cold and wet most of the year – the riding will warm us up. It doesn't matter that the national dish of bacon and cabbage followed by custard means that we haven't traditionally had the tautest of abs – sure, the riding will tone us right up a treat.

There is no pressure here: we only have to be sexy like our own selves. If you don't have someone to do it with, do it with yourself (see Chapter 77). If you don't like it, don't do it. But don't be ashamed. I swear you'll feel better, more at ease, more dynamic at work, play, or at overthrowing an ineffective government. It's always been fun, but right now it's vital that everyone living in this country who wants to gets on board the riding train.

Remember. We're doing it for Ireland. What have we got to lose?

45

SEE IT. SMASH IT. BURN IT.

Remember when I wrote about white privilege in Chapter 41? It might be useful to read that piece again. I'll wait. Done? Good, thank you. Not sorry.

Much of what that piece covers works for any kind of privilege. In it, I refer to privilege as a veil being lifted, blinkers coming off. It's exciting to see it happen for men with regard to sexism, as it sometimes does whenever there's a high profile sexual assault case. (Note: when this was written, we had no idea of what 2017 in terms of the post-Weinstein, #metoo flood would bring – good and all as my predictions are.)

What happens when someone is sexually assaulted? Well, usually, barely there sentencing happens. The important thing is to favour a grand lad and his possible future, with barely a nod to the life and future of the survivor, now changed forever. There are victim impact statements. Condemnation from all but the perpetrator's closest associates. Appeals for calm, 'Was it really that bad?' And the sickening knowledge that these cases are not isolated, not rare.

Women nod angrily, wearily. We know this (#metoo). We're supposed to put up with the lack of justice for sexual assault. We're supposed to accept the possibility of those assaults and guard against them because they will somehow be our fault. We are repeatedly told – in anything from a roar to the constant low hum every woman hears – that we are expendable, props in a theatrical piece playing out with only leading men. That it's possible – probable – to hurt us and get away with it. That this is just the way things are. What a weird system.

But then, many couldn't hold it in any more. Distantly, separately, a counter-roar began as countless women shared stories of everyday demeaning, belittling, groping and more serious attacks. Because we all have those stories. #yesallwomen. Yes #metoo. Even powerful ones. They called on the great men in our lives to stop supporting from the back and be the advance patrol; to help create a culture of mutual respect where violent assaults might become less likely in the first place. Sadly, #notallmen got on board. But the ones who did made us fierce excited altogether. Especially here in Ireland, where male privilege was stamped so heavily into our constitution with big 1930s boots. No wonder some lads are still so banterific, still believe it's their birthright to have their dinner cooked by an apron-wearing virgin: the inequality of women is in our very laws. Privilege, consent and autonomy are inextricably linked.

Soon, we hear, there will be robots, like in *Humans*, who can service people sexually from a state of perma-consent. (Though maybe you should still check to see if the robot is up for it. Maybe you should still check that the robot is turned on.) Until technology catches up, we need to get the word out into lad world that women are not punchlines, distractions, toys. We are not games consoles. We are not vessels. We need lads' help to spread that word from the inside.

One International Men's Day, I made the lamest joke on social media. It wasn't even funny, but you see, I don't find this system funny at all. It was something like 'Happy IMD! I wish men twenty-four hours of being treated the same as women!' And in they swooped. Dive-bombed. The ones who love the feel of their blinkers and who say we're making it all up. They told me I hated men. I was trampling on their day, *their one day, their special day!* I was pro-male suicide and depression. I was a denier of domestic violence against men. I was the worst – you wouldn't even find my slimy trail on the sole of a heavy 1930s boot. But not one of them campaigned on any of these extremely serious issues (I checked). Not one of them mentioned any of the above any other day of the year, just wheeled them out whenever someone made a lame joke at the expense of a system that means that every day is International Men's Day. The system screws you over too, blinkered swoopers; it's the very thing making you feel so hard done by that you can't take a (stupid, lame) joke. That system is a lie, tricking us all. Why not help us burn it down? We'll bring marshmallows.

We know this now, right? Privilege (or lack thereof) means we don't get where we are (wherever we are) on our own. Its influence is everywhere: in films, comics, bad jokes, games; for every Lara Croft there are a hundred peasant girls or sex workers running, pleading, scared. Female tropes are either disposable hags dispensing wisdom or sexy faery warriors dispensing sex. Or dead. Often dead.

Misogyny is the go-to put-down for any woman who puts her head above the parapet. *What is she wearing? Did you hear her whiny voice? Isn't she fat/old/slutty?* Mate, we can wear what we want, eat what we want, have all the sex we want so long as it's consensual, so long as it's safe. And, just so you know, 'woman' is not an insult.

Many lads are stepping up. More than I ever remember. But imagine if all the lads saw what we see? Imagine if they all began to understand? Imagine if that led them to like, *like* us? We could hang out all night long, toasting marshmallows. If that happened, the rubbish system would be fucked. Not sorry.

46

SHAME

So, shame.

Irish people – women in particular – aren't having it any more. Just like that. We're not having it.

Some people seem to think some genitals are better than others: that penises are akin to the fiery swords of archangels, genitals of the righteous. (Whip it out on a battlefield, though, and I'm not sure it's as powerful as they imagine.)

There's no one correct set of genitals. Innies, outies, unique and in between – none is inherently more shameful or pride-inducing than the other. Ditto what you choose to do with them in private.

So you can't use my genitals to shame me. Because they're great! I'm not boasting, they're probably only grand, but I like them and whether I open or close my legs is my business. But don't let that stop shamers thinking incessantly about them and trying – bless them – to make sex or sex organs embarrassing for me. Can't be done. Sorry. I love 'em. Mmm, mmm can't get me enough of that good stuff. And wondering whether those shamers would take or leave my stuff takes up zero minutes of my day.

One of my favourite wannabe abusive messages was this (I assume it was meant for a forum rather than my inbox but I don't think brightness is this person's top attribute): 'That one!' (i.e. me) 'I heard she had sex with loads of comedians.' Do you mean I was single and working with other single people and sometimes we ended up hooking up? Well, cuff me and take me away! Newsflash: when you're single and work with people for years, stuff might happen. Healthy, normal stuff. Enjoyable too. How is that embarrassing? Unless you think sex itself is embarrassing (how's that working out for your pants?) or … and I'm sorry, I'm leaning towards this … you've come here in a time machine from the 1950s and still believe that men having sex are legends and women who have it are sluts. Ahhh, pet. We're not having that any more.

I once saw someone tweet the Abortion Rights Campaign that women 'all want filled with the penis', which – apart from the erasure of those women for whom such filling isn't a turn on – it seems he saw as a bad thing. There's nothing wrong with a good filling, sir! He went on: 'vile women murdering the unborn' … 'god forbid your [sic] filled with a child'. In other words, the filling itself is not shameful so long as the intended outcome is motherhood.

There's a lot to unpack here and I don't want to take up too much of your day, but the reduction of woman to receptacle – penis receiver, baby deliverer – can't be lost on you. The not-so-subtle message that women come in two flavours: good and bad. Bad, shameful women all simply gagging for the writer's giant, throbbing, righteous archangel member, not even having the decency to feel guilty about their desires, while good, shame-free women only have sex with the intention of becoming mothers. How many times would that be in a lifetime? Maximum twenty, at the outside? These are unacceptably low goals, sir!

Some people don't enjoy sex or want to have it with only one partner ever; there's room for all of us in this crazy, sexy world. No judgement here whether you wish never to have it or you're having it right now, balancing your tablet on a dildo. So long as you're doing it (or not doing it) safely, don't let anyone shame you for it.

At Dublin Comedy Improv, 'dildo' or 'vibrator' are suggestions we get every week. Every single week, accompanied by a snigger because they're inherently hilarious, apparently. That makes our job very easy, if all we have to do is say a word. Who needs a sketch?

You should see the reaction to 'gynaecologist'. People shout these particular suggestions up to try to throw us – they think we'll be too embarrassed to touch them. But you've come to the wrong show if you think we won't touch dildos. Dildos don't scare us. Throw your dildos at us all you like.

So off back to the fifties with you and your perceived superiority and shame. Those bashful days are done. But tell you what, sir: we'd love a go of your time machine.

47

NICENESS

'Niceness' has become a dirty word. An insult. The Muddening is partly to blame and it's a shame, because niceness is a useful way to navigate the outside world when we leave our caves, without clubbing everyone else on the head. If we all vented every single time we felt annoyance, or even antipathy, in the face of human interaction, there'd be a lot more throbbing craniums and we'd never get anything done. Sometimes it's more productive to smile and nod and GTFO.

So how do you do that – i.e. bite your tongue to avoid unnecessary conflict – and still end up saying what you mean? Tricky. To be honest, I'm not sure it can be done. But choosing battles, saving your caveperson club for the big ones, is more valuable than constant clubbing over every point.

I don't know about you, but I spend a lot of my time biting my tongue, forcing a grin, or banging hard on my desk with clenched fists. On the phone, I'll hold the handset at arm's length away from my ear and count to ten, allowing imaginary cartoon steam to escape my ears. There isn't a swear word my neighbours haven't heard me scream at the top of my lungs in frustration, especially when directed at late night TV panel shows. And nothing – nothing makes me screamier than inequality.

Tantrums are only cute when you're three. You can stamp your foot and pull your hair out then and voice your displeasure all you want and people just put videos of you on Facebook, charged with being 'totes adorbs'. After three, though, *totes adorbs* can turn to *self-absorbed* and is most definitely not cute. It is instead a terrible use of our time.

Holding back can make for good strategy. Sincerity is wonderful and to be prized in this post-fact world, but if we don't choose where and when to drop it, we're in danger of spending it all on petty shit. I'm not talking about lying – even the little white ones, which some advocate – I'm talking simply buttoning it occasionally: not losing the rag over every single thing, even if that's a pain in the arse. It involves a bit of omission, yes, but no misleading.

This becomes especially pertinent when you have something important to say, say on another's behalf, or with a goal in mind, and when others are out to contradict you as you do so. Anyone who canvassed or campaigned during the run up to the Marriage Equality referendum knows what I mean. Part of being heard means you need to keep people listening; no one likes being shouted at – especially on their front porch. They switch off. Doors shut in your face. It may make you dig your nails into your palms (mine are red raw), but sometimes choosing more measured language than 'You're a horrible liar and I hate you' gets you closer to where you need to be, even if 'You're a horrible liar and I hate you' is what you've embroidered onto the pillow you're going to punch later.

If you always go in all guns blazing, you're left with nowhere to go. This will become evident as the momentum to repeal the Eighth Amendment builds; many of us with lived experience are already burning out. We must keep our heads. We must hold. Hold. For now.

Eventually, there will be no option but for the gloves to come off. There will come a time. If you've been biding yours, then you'll know. Not having wasted your 'liars' or 'disgustings' or 'viles', they can now have impact if they really have to be unleashed. And I'm sure it will feel so bloody good. Believe me, my head reaches near exploding point several times a day and I've no doubt that at some stage it'll happen in circumstances I can't control. Till then, I don't want to give anyone campaigning for me to not have rights the satisfaction of it. But if you'd like to know how I really feel, maybe just picture a small, Cork-formed mushroom cloud. A mushroom cloud with a fringe. That's why it galls me when those not involved dispense tone-policing advice: as if we haven't thought of strategy. As if we aren't polite. As if we aren't already biting our tongues, holding in mushroom-cloud level rage in the face of often brutal abuse. We know, lads, thanks.

We know that if the pressure valve is always fully opened you are bound to run out of steam. And you're no good to anyone steamless, least of all yourself. So, 'I just want to help you reach the middle ground' folk: we have thought of all this. We're already doing it. Our tongues are nearly bitten through.

It does amuse me to see 'niceness' sit alongside 'P.C.' or 'vegetarian', on the insult shelf. 'Nice' now means vanilla, boring, fence-sitting, cowardly, lacking in edge. What next? 'Soft'? 'Kind'? 'Non-violent'? 'You people sicken me, not clubbing everyone to a pulp on sight. Don't you care? Hypocrites! Monsters!'

Keeping your powder dry is an excellent military term that should appeal to the Not Nice (I'm guessing that's what they want to be called) but there are a lot of spit flecks landing on it, is all I'm saying. We're going to need it later. Hold.

Besides, is anyone really naïve enough to think people are really nice? Take a look around you. Anyone with eyes can see we're all awful.

48

SHOUT YOUR CHOICE

I'd like to explore the tone-policing stuff a little further. I'm still not over it. (What a shock, says you.) This piece aims to tease out some of the common criticisms head-on.

We find ourselves at a moment when Ireland is finally waking up to the fact that it's done wrong by its daughters, sisters and mothers for far too long. A time of almost too many actions declaring this wrong-doing to list: testimonies, jumpers, murals, donuts, short films, investigative journalism, memorials, badges, protests, songs, talks. We're talking now, our way. And we're angry.

But naturally some people don't like it.

There have been the usual attempts to shut the conversation down, including some rather bizarre attempts to muddy the water.

I have been called *shrill* when actually I've got quite a deep man's voice to go with my hairiness. The powerful video of Sarah Griffin's poem *We Face This Land* had some big thinkers taking down how we looked, saying we were demon-like, fat, witches (thank you). But remember, lads: we're already biting our tongues. We're already being polite, respectful, creative. If you're focusing on the delivery of the message, not the message, it's clearly the message you have a problem with. It's almost as if you'd prefer … wait a second … almost as if you'd prefer we'd shut up again! Hmmm.

Have I seen pro-choice people get angry? In the face of lies and horrible personal stuff being thrown at them, yes, justifiably so. In fact, most have handled it with grace and humour. Please don't confuse *insistent, determined, confident* for *aggressive*. Still I see a kind of myth evolving of extreme and aggressive pro-choice campaigners, and how we should modify our message to be just a teensy bit more anti-choice to reach people who are confused. More confusion to ease confusion? Sounds great! I'm sure that would be really effective. Muddening, how are you?

The only way to combat confusion is with fact. Sometimes, for 'balance', a broadcaster is forced to sit on actual facts when faced with a stream of misinformation poured from someone in a suit. Please, broadcasters and journalists: your homework on this will have to be airtight. Get it done, I beg you. And listeners, just because someone is wearing a suit does not mean they're truthful. Remember the banks?

Certain anti-choice campaigners deliberately mislead. But we're extreme.

They say 'Adoption is always an option', whereas we condemn coercion, whether it's to end or continue a pregnancy, or give a baby up for adoption. But we're extreme.

They speak of those who regret, when apparently ninety-five per cent do not. Regarding the five per cent who do, I cannot even imagine their pain. But how much of their regret is due to stigma and lack of support? To then wheel them out to bolster a campaign to criminalise them is, in my view, really inappropriate, definitely not compassionate. But we're extreme.

But you have to engage with the fact that it ends a life!

We do. All the time. Potential for life, anyway. We also acknowledge that ninety per cent of abortions happen pre-thirteen weeks. And that after that it's almost always a wanted pregnancy gone tragically, medically wrong.

Everyone is entitled to their beliefs and many of us don't believe that life begins at conception. Potential for life, sure. But early term abortions (the majority, unless there are serious medical complications) are, to many, still only potential for life. In a wanted pregnancy or according to certain religious beliefs, people project personhood onto a developing foetus. This is a lovely thing. But it is not everyone's experience.

For that reason, recourse must be to medical facts and terms. We don't 'shy away' from saying 'baby'; in most cases 'embryo' or 'foetus' are the appropriate medical terms.

Does abortion end this developing potential for life? Yes. You know who knows that better than anyone? Someone who's wrestled with the decision when faced with a crisis pregnancy and found, after serious reflection, that they – we – are okay morally with what needs to happen. Consider this: people who believe in life from conception sometimes need abortions too. We support them in what must be an unbelievably painful decision.

Many of us speaking publicly have lived experience. We don't want to relive a procedure that was part of a traumatic time step by step and in glorious technicolour because you demand it, if that's all right with you.

Yet we are extreme.

Well, if we are extreme, we're extreme about butting out of other people's medical business.

We are extreme about understanding that if you aren't living someone's life you can't know what they are able for, or expect them to do what you might.

We are extremely mad about medical facts. Mmm, we gobble that peer-reviewed research right up.

We are extreme about saying that our own beliefs can't be imposed on everyone else.

But you are right: we extremely refuse to be silent, or told *how* to conduct a conversation that affects us directly, that is ours to have. Until we did, no one did, and we're not going back to that. That's an extreme 'no' from us.

Those who try to reduce this to some kind of genteel debate, a black and white issue, clearly have little understanding of the complex realities at hand. And the privilege, *the sheer, blissful luxury*, of being able to theorise about it at a remove … This is happening every day, to people you know. Indulge in philosophical intellectual raptures in the drawing room over cigars. We're getting on planes or boats, or bleeding.

The facts might make you uncomfortable, but how they are delivered doesn't change them. We are angry. It's right to be angry about this. We will cry at the top of our lungs for our rights, we will laugh at how ridiculous it is that we must, we will scream till you hear us.

Listen. Listen. Listen.

49

UNBRIDLED ANGER MANAGEMENT

And speaking of anger ...

When I started writing the column for HeadStuff 'Rage-In' seemed like a good title. A hook to hang the pieces on and a solid – if not *amazing* – pun. I am often raging. Having a weekly rage-in seemed apt.

The only problem is, I'm not always angry. Sometimes, I have had quite a good week and it's hard to find something to push back against (though admittedly, this is rare).

I do have a sort of background seethe level, bubbling away, but I try to address what makes me angry in real life as it occurs. That tends to allow the anger to dissipate. Stops it pooling and swirling and threatening to boil over. So I don't always feel angry enough to be *really* angry enough to write about it every week. I have too much faith in humanity – even the dicks. Dicks are only looking for attention, after all. Dicks are sad. Sometimes I just want to give them a cuddle. Not a long one. Not a very deep one. But a cuddle, nonetheless. And then take a quick plunge in some disinfectant sheep-dip.

There's power in using anger constructively. Sometimes it's right and just. It doesn't mean you're uncivil or out of control. It means you're angry. But some people still have a problem when women do it. Some people still wish it was 1649.

Back in witch-hunting times, women who voiced anger were persecuted as 'scolds'. There were actual legal provisions for this. Scolds might be threatened with having spikes driven through their tongues – if they were lucky enough not to be decreed full witches (witches were also scolds; it was part of the package) and tossed onto a bonfire or drowned. The crime of being a scold – a troublesome, shrewish or angry woman – was punishable by humiliation in the stocks or use of devices such as the *scold's bridle*, a kind of cage or mask worn over the face with a piece fitted inside the mouth, to silence them. Or they might be sat on ducking stools and dunked in the nearest river. Not full drowning, you understand: just a refreshing dip to bring her to her senses. (There were practically no male scolds, lads; no bridles for you. Sorry if that's the sort of thing you're into.) In *Crime, Gender and Social Order in Early Modern England*, Garthine Walker states that a scold was 'any woman offering an opinion' or 'any woman who verbally resisted or flouted authority publicly and stubbornly enough to challenge the underlying dictum of male rule' which, outside of her household, made her 'socially dangerous'. Female passivity was so prized that there were laws and torture to ensure that passivity was upheld. *Smile, luv, that ducking might never happen.*

There are no such overt methods of dealing with us pesky, nagging harridans any more, worse luck, but it's clear that women being angry are still unpalatable. So we get ducked verbally. We're *a bit of a holy show. A disgrace. Wild, unreasonable. Disordered* and creating disorder wherever we go. It's a shame. There's something glorious about justified anger, well vented. Jesus got mad in the temple: He turned over tables and everything. He let fly at the money changers and profiteers. He didn't hold back. He wasn't meek, blessed though that would have made Him. Thank His Dad he wasn't a woman, or many people who wish we'd shut up might have had to make do with some very different role models. We'd probably never have heard of Jesusina, except maybe as a cautionary tale of what happens when women go off the rails in markets: bad things – ridicule, infamy. Maybe even accusations of insanity. An ol' stoning. Either way, there wouldn't be a whole testament dedicated to her every move and word, the mad harpy.

I'm not always raging. There's plenty to make me content with my lot: family, friends, cat videos, my actual cat, *Catfish*, dogs, work, chipper chips, hot water in shower form, exercise, some books, good WiFi, wine and open fires. Pretty much in that order too. But if given cause, I will not be ashamed of my anger. I will not rein it in for your comfort – because what is giving me cause is causing me much greater discomfort. I do not always smile. I will not always smile. I like to smile, smiling's pleasant, it feels good, but it's not my job. You know who always smiles? Greeters in restaurants. I am not showing you to a table, not today. If ever I am and I don't smile, please feel free not to tip. Today, I am not asking for crumbs of approval, nor do I accept them: I'm not looking for approval at all. If I raise my voice, I'm looking to be heard. Got it? Good. It's what Jesusina would have wanted.

50

WAX ON, WAX OFF

Intermission –

I'm led into the torture chamber. A tiny cubicle. Clinical. There is a bed, some tools, a heating device. What horrors has this room known? Fluorescent-lit and stark, only a curtain separates it from the world outside. It is a room each woman must enter alone, every six weeks or so, depending on stubble regrowth rate. For it is waxing time.

My tiny torturer dispenses the first and perhaps worst of the torments: I must put a pair of paper knickers on. This initial degradation is clearly meant to break me, and prevent me from running away. You wouldn't be caught dead at home in these saggy baggy yokes, let alone in the centre of a capital city. This is only the beginning: the humiliation will intensify, and the pain is yet to come. In the heating device, the wax is bubbling up.

I long to cry out to the sky, visible through the skylight directly above me – birds, freer now than I (and allowed to keep their feathers). When bears and horses strut about, we speak of glossy coats, of shiny manes, of luscious whiskers on the neighbour's cat. But I must rip my whiskers out, or be deemed 'unfeminine' or worse, 'ungroomed'. Surely grooming would be to keep the whiskers on, give them a brush and show them off?

In the fluorescent cubicle, hot molten wax is poured onto my upper thigh for somewhere between one second and forever; I can't tell. My senses blur, all energies converge at my nerve endings and I MUST NOT SCREAM because they'll know. *They'll know.*

They'll have won: they'll have been right, they told me so – not doing this regularly means it's so much sorer when you do come back.

While the warrior-woman tears follicle and flesh from my lower limbs, I wonder why I am so weak? Why do I give in, come here at all? Why do I not let my leg hair grow and flap majestically in the breeze? It's the same hair as on my head, no? Why is its grossness dependent on its position on my body? If you tied a scarf around your head or around your knee, it'd still be a scarf: no one would look at your knee scarf and cry 'Eww! Disgusting!'; they'd recognise it as a scarf. They'd know that its position further down the body doesn't change its molecular structure, rendering it a disgusto-scarf.

I wish I were a stronger woman. I wish I could withstand irrational cries of 'Eww', save some euros and just let my hair flow free.

Perhaps, like Samson, if we let our woman hair grow our strength would be even mightier. But I will never know for I am weak. I believed those razor ads where women threw scarves down their legs (still regular scarves, despite not being in the head and neck area); good women's scarves slid all the way down and bad women's scarves snagged on disgusting, disgusting stubble. Meanwhile, over in men's ads, a lad with stubble would rub his roguish chin and say 'I'm rugged and I know it' with his eyes.

But I am weak and – though I don't cry out – I let them scald my legs and I pay them for it. I could melt down old Christmas candles at home and save a fortune, but this is a kind of pain that sanity insists one not inflict upon oneself. Home waxing is a bridge too far.

I bite my lip. I wince. I gasp. I try to keep up conversation and pretend that all of this is normal. And I am doomed, for Mediterranean complexioned as I am, the regrowth will be sprouting before my silly paper pants have hit the bin. I will leave the shopping centre with unrugged disgusting stubble. In two weeks, I'm back to being a carpet-in-training.

And further to the weakness – I enjoy a smooth leg. I like the air to touch my skin. I like that skin to gleam. I reserve the right to someday throw a scarf down it for some reason and not have it snag. I like to wave at people and not have my underarm fuzz obscure my face. *I'm over here!* But you won't know that if I don't defuzz.

The torturer rips off not just cooling wax but a layer of my feminism. I wish I could let it all grow in and proudly wear it out instead of socks. But I am weak. So weak.

Those of you who do not wax or clip or trim their way to conformity, I salute you. You are my hairoines. I am not among your much more confident number.

And though I manage not to let on that I'm in pain, it's clear that if I ever found myself in an actual torture situation, I'd sing like a hairy canary. The wax is not the real torture, the pressure is. And I've let everyone down.

51

WE ARE MONSTERS

I am a monster. You are a monster. Someone somewhere is hunting us. They are asking where we live and they are coming to put us out of our misery. Because we make them miserable. We are the foundation of their woes. We deserve whatever we get, what they're about to give us. The world will be better without us in it. Because we are monsters.

Dehumanising is a powerful tool. My husband and I sometimes discuss the ways in which we've experienced it used against each of us. The ways are different, the results the same; people take the goodness from us so we can be monsters to them, all the better for them to hate us.

He is a black man. To some this means 'wild', 'savage', 'more prone to violent tendencies'. He is, to them, a kind of animal. A barely civilised beast, because of the colour of his skin.

I, meanwhile, am hardly of nature at all. I do not have and did not want children. When I had a crisis pregnancy, I chose to end it. So I am 'unnatural', 'cold', 'inhumane', even 'inhuman'. To those who would steal our humanity to prove their point, we are nothing more than creatures. They are certain about this. They want others to think it too.

Removing someone's humanity makes cruelty easier. Like hurling insults around the world from the comfort of a keyboard, behind the shield of anonymity. These warriors don't lose sleep, pricked with guilt because they have unsettled someone – hurt them, even – from a thousand miles away. To them, we're not people. We're just a game.

Women who are assertive and clear are 'shrill and shrieking Feminazis'. Like birds, we are, or pterodactyls, maybe, squawking, flapping and functioning only on base, irrational instinct. Or organised and heartless, like villains in a war film.

We are 'bints' or 'cunts', 'beaver', 'pussy'. 'Vaginas on legs'. Where did the rest of us go?

Over the centuries, Irish people have been labelled 'pigs', 'drunks', 'ape-like', 'stupid'. These generalisations helped some to justify treating us badly, even to the point of letting us starve.

The homeless are not merely unlucky, they are a different kind of person altogether. A kind from whom it is all right to turn a blind eye. The Travelling Community are not to be trusted. Muslims are suspicious. Refugees and those in Direct Provision – *why are they here? What do they want? My job? I don't know a thing about them.* That's if they reach here. We don't seem to be making it easy and it doesn't look like heading 'back where you came from' is possible. Syria is on fire. Now what?

Drone strikes make dropping bombs more palatable because the bomber isn't even there. Moving dots on a screen barely elicit a second thought, let alone an emotional response. (If they did, the next big blockbuster would be *Moving Dots on a Screen.* You wouldn't even have to cut back to shots of some guy with a conscience. It would be cheap to make and a giant hit.)

I can barely think about the tendency towards dehumanisation of minorities across the world, and where that might lead, let alone write about it. This is about so much more than offence.

Once society agrees on othering as a tool – 'They're not like us.' 'Nothing to do with me!' – and it isn't addressed, you have no control of what direction it will take. Once we decide someone – anyone – is lesser, anything can happen. And who knows when you might become 'other'. Depends on what they need. If that's how we agree to operate, then all they have to do is pretend you're not like them and BAM: you're the monster.

Of course, none of us are monsters. We have a chance now not to contribute to the advance of monstrous things. Perhaps there won't be a world war; I hope with all my heart there won't be devastation on that scale. But already, the first step to violence, to depriving others of their rights and dignity, to pain, is in place. People have already been harmed. As damaging: their real and constant fear. Living with that is a kind of violence too.

So, maybe don't mock minorities by having hilarious racists on your TV or radio show. Remind the lads that rape isn't funny. Look into people's eyes and remember that they're you. Don't think things are all that bad? Don't think it will affect you? It's time to look past our own spheres – bubbles, if you will. True, the marginalised will be worst affected. But if you think this will not touch you or change something fundamental in all of our lives, your bubble might be about to burst. And if we have reached a point where we only speak up against hate if it affects us directly, it is already too late.

If we don't repair the disconnect now, it's our own humanity that will have been lost. Then monsters will have got us.

52

DEAR FELLOW FEMINAZIS

I write this from The Bunker (you know where, *wink wink*). All is in readiness.

But, my fellow Feminazis, they are on to us. The only surprise is how long it has taken those of such Superior Intellect and Understanding to discover our takeover plans and that their very superiority – and therefore self-worth – is under attack. By us. Just 'cos. For we are awful. (As you know, Being Awful is Point 1 in the Feminazi Manifesto.)

How do we know they are on to us? They are angry. Just look at all the tweets and thinkpieces hurtling at us, smug and fast. Make sure you're ready to duck at all times, like we practised at Secret Feminazi Bootcamp. If a thinkpiece lands right, it could take your eye out.

Perhaps, in hindsight, 'Feminazi' wasn't the most sympathetic choice of title, but the Superiors came up with it so it must be right. They are right about so much, but WE MUST NOT LET ON THAT THEY ARE. Like how we made rape culture up: we are playing a seriously long game on this one, by letting ourselves get assaulted and having the judicial system pretend it's all a laugh. On top of this, no one known to Superiors *looks* like a rapist. Rapists, as we all know, are distinguishable by their humps, stovepipe hats, snarling expressions, great mutton chop facial hair and dark alley-dwelling habits. No one's seen one of these for decades, so rape is obviously makey-uppy, just as stats show many Irish people believe consent to be.[1] Perhaps the most despicable part of our despicable

---

1   According to a recent survey twenty-one per cent of Irish people believe

plan is making people aware of the threat we feel much of the time, backed up by facts. *So evil.* And, as Being Evil is Point 2 on the Feminazi Manifesto, let's call this progress.

The Superiors are also right to say we are not victims: when something bad happens to us we are, in fact, 'people-to-whom-something-has-happened-but-if-the-Superiors-didn't-do-it-personally-or-see-it-happen-then-stop-being-so-dramatic-and-shut-up'. We're just not grateful enough for them, or something, whatever. But letting them focus on what they perceive to be our victimhood suits our cause perfectly. Blinded by Superior Intellect and Much Thinking, they miss our many traps. Like how their repeatedly opining about our 'whining' while doing nothing to change anything is actually whining! Crying victim, you might say! Ironic. ('Irony' seems to be a word with which they struggle. Henceforth, let irony be our code.)

They seem to think this is all about holding doors open or mad things like that. Let them be distracted by this as tiny kittens are by yarn. Of course, we all hold doors open for people of all genders and none, unless we have a boiling hot coffee in hand. We rarely stop and check whether the other person has a penis. But the Superiors tell us doorways are THE MAIN BATTLEGROUND. Stay woke at entrances and exits. And remember, what one Feminazi does is indicative of every single other woman in the world. ALL FEMINISTS HATE ALL MEN. I was just saying this to my husband. We have only not studied Men Hating at Bootcamp because we didn't think of it. However the Superiors keep saying it so we must relent and include it in our Manifesto. Point 3.

Fellow Feminazis, never let them realise that so many of you

---

having sex without consent is justified in certain situations. No, I can't believe it, either.

are men. For now, the Superiors seem completely unaware of this, even as a possibility. They think feminism is the sole preserve of unreasonable women. Good work, team.

One of our main quests is to have a say in what happens to our own bodies, even though we can't possibly know what to do with them. When Superiors are not present, we are forever falling down, cutting ourselves on nothing and hurling ourselves into barrels of salt, for some reason. We would only let autonomy go to our heads and become crazed with it. Like our secret plan to make everyone have compulsory abortions (even though we have literally nothing to gain from that): those of us who have had them want everyone to enjoy the trauma and extra expense instead of using contraception *WHICH ALWAYS WORKS* because we are such shits. (Manifesto Point 4.)

Last Bootcamp, Jacinta brought up some excellent points. 'Isn't there a male suicide epidemic?' she asked. 'Don't men suffer violence too? Aren't some fathers not granted fair access to their kids?' Yes, these are true. And though our campaigning tackles the very patriarchal system that creates such negative situations for all genders, we must let them say we don't care. That our lady brains can only process one thing at a time, that we only care about things that affect us directly. Us being portrayed simplistically as villains is vital to our cover. Do not blow it, bitches!

Next week's Secret Feminazi Training Camp will focus on career, which is, of course, being Feminazis. It's a full-time job for life.

The chosen camp biscuits will be the chocolate covered Kimberley kind as these are soft, which is a nice balance to our hardness.

Make sure your boots are shiny, thigh-high and hurty.

Yours in thick, whiny, faux-victimhood (god their whining's getting boring).

Feminazi Flynn.

53

ONE POINTED ATTENTION
— ON SINGLE ISSUE CAMPAIGNING

Women are reputed to be great multi-taskers and I guess, for the most part, it's true. I never come downstairs without bringing a load of washing, taking two steps at a time with the phone cradled snugly between ear and shoulder, as I calmly beg someone at the other end for work. I always try to bust out some squats and crunches while I watch *Real Housewives of Wherever*. I'm eating a banana as I type this. You get the picture.

But I've been to yoga classes (you can't say I haven't, I mentioned it earlier, remember?) and I know about one-pointed attention. Mindfulness. It's where you set your vision, outer and inner (stay with me), on one point. You bring your wandering monkey-mind back when it strays off. You meditate. It stills you, helps you cope; problems feel less daunting or maybe even easier to solve afterwards. If you'll allow me to get all hippy-dippy for a second (like I hadn't already; too late to back out now, mo'fo's!), if you're not focused, you're not present. You're supposedly not truly living. *Baha! Just kidding.* But no, seriously: you're living, only sloppily.

I agree with the view that although the rash of doing-things-while-doing-other-things makes us *feel* productive and busy, it actually means we're not doing any one thing well. It means we're half-arsing, even as we feel we're double-jobbing. It wears us out and spreads us so thin that you might as well nickname us *I Can't Believe We're Not Better*.

Doing your homework down the back of the bus isn't the best

way to really learn anything. It makes your handwriting all scrawly and illegible and ties the rest of your senses up, so you might not even know if someone wanted to get off with you. (I still associate the back of buses with snogging. It makes for some uncomfortable late-night journeys.) What I'm saying is obvious: you retain very little when you're not concentrating. It's why we switch off social media when we're working. Don't we? *We all switch it off, right? Guys? Hello?*

When addressing something as serious as campaigning for rights, it's important to put everything you have into it. I remember a chat I had with myself as the Marriage Equality campaign hotted up. I don't have many chats with myself, so it must have been important. (This is a lie: I talk to myself all day long.) Anyway, I said, 'Tara, LGBT citizens shouldn't have to ask for equality, but they do, for some mad reason most people have forgotten at this stage. It's your duty to get out there and do everything you can to help them ask, and tell people why you believe they shouldn't have to, so saying *No* makes no sense. Got that, Tara? Put down that remote. Listen up, biatch: leave everything on the pitch. Have no regrets. This is not a dress rehearsal. Don't wake up the day after the referendum and think "I wish I'd done just one more thing." You want to wake up and say, "We won." But even if we don't, FOR CHRIST'S SAKE DON'T let it be for want of you doing that one more thing.'

After telling myself there was no need to shout at me, I let it sink in. I did everything I could think of, every day in the run-up. It was selfish really, I suppose; insuring against my own feeling bad at the end of it all. But I did what I suggested and every time I felt like not having a conversation, or not canvassing, or not contributing in other ways available to me, I shook me and reminded me of the conversation with me. It became almost a full-time job, by the end.

I can only imagine what it was like for frontline campaigners. I listened to what they were telling me, tried to do what they asked. I tried to think of other ways to push on. I watched a nation get focused and pull together and something wonderful happened.

Of course, there were obstacles. Not just the inevitable ones – those from the No camp. Distraction can come from surprising quarters. In fact, that's possibly the biggest thing the Marriage Equality campaign taught me. And one of the favoured distractions (apart from unending tone policing) was 'whataboutery'.

Why are you all giving this campaign your focus when there are homeless children on the streets? Who cares who can marry whom when unemployment is ravishing the land? What about charges/taxes/poverty/trolleys in hospital corridors? Or, my favourite: *What about Repeal the Eighth?*

Reader: 'Urgh, not again. Is she talking about it *again*?'

Hey, it wasn't me this time! I didn't bring it up, it was the Marriage Referendum whatabouterers! Bet they're sorry now! Was there ever a bit of the constitution you were more sick of hearing about? Well ya know who's sickest of it? Us. Because, as we now know, many of the people who actively campaigned for MarRef ended up at the forefront of the campaign to repeal the Eighth. We don't bang on about it because it's fun, or trendy, or cool. It's not. It's tiring and repetitive and we all have plenty else we'd rather be doing going on in our lives. I like dogs, trash TV and long walks on the beach, myself.

So, it turns out, my whatabouty friends, that we were concerned about the Eighth, but we focused on MarRef till it got done. With every campaign, every issue, while sideline commentators try to dissipate this focus – for reasons best known to themselves –

campaigners get their heads down and their hands dirty. Funny, I haven't seen many of those whatabouterers who asked why we were ignoring repeal out once repeal became the thing on the agenda.

It's short-sighted to assume that campaigners on one issue don't see other problems, or aren't working away on them, quietly. Maybe they see how many rights and freedoms correlate, intersect, and are merely prioritising one area first, to make others easier. In the case of repeal, full reproductive choice could lead to better care for existing children and families hit hardest by poverty. Migrant women and those in Direct Provision here, with their added visa complications, have more difficulty in accessing abortion than most. Even more fundamentally, without autonomy none of us is free. And without this most basic freedom, you have nothing.

Repeal of the Eighth Amendment might not be what you would prioritise, but I've lived its effects. Exile isn't exactly the craic and I see real misogyny at the amendment's core that reaches much further into our society than reproductive rights alone. That's why some whatabouterers will work pretty hard to *whatabout* repeal campaigners. It seems misogyny's grand to them. So we have lots to do.

Ireland has come a long way. It's a young, progressive country and has a chance to lead the way in terms of human rights. But there's still plenty of inequality we can work on. Repeal is the one I'm focusing on. Like a kitty with a laser pointer, I'm on it. Chasing it, even when it drives me up the wall. You're free to campaign on whatever you like – in fact, that's often how these things work best. You work on that, I'll work on this. '*Start with a shitcorner … etc.*' Me? I want to leave everything on that pitch.

54

STOP, LOOK, LISTEN

This was my last weekly column for HeadStuff. I left leaving anyone who wanted to take part in the Repeal campaign some thoughts and homework, if they were up for it. I wanted to group some recurring points in one, easy-reference package. It's a kind of summing up, but also an invitation to reflect. So if campaigning's not for you, please feel free to skip to another section.

We keep hearing how tricky it's going to be to have conversations in the run-up to a referendum. Well, I've been having every version of the conversation for ages now, so here's a handy guide to how to keep yourself safe, without getting run over by myths, lie-juggernauts and people who haven't really thought the route through but are intent on running you off it, even though they don't have a licence themselves and prefer to sit down the back of the bus, in a most pass-remarkable way, while somebody else does the driving. (You didn't think I'd let my last column go without an overworked extended metaphor, now did you?)

Sadly, we need to forget most media reporting on this. They tie themselves into such knots striving for 'balance' that balance is the last thing they provide. Giving fifty per cent of airtime to myth is not balance. On top of that, their thirst for two warring sides robs the discussion of nuance when, in fact, nuance is all there is. This has never been black and white. Now, ignoring the media is going to be hard, because that's how many people get their info. So, we need to give those people a dig out. Make sure they have access to facts, make sure they're asking the right questions. Because this isn't about not having questions or doubts, it's about not being dragged down a rabbit hole about views on abortion (we will never all agree) or on when life begins (if science can't find consensus, we eejits never will).

I find it useful to stay focused on a few simple facts. Here are the main ones:

We all know someone who's had an abortion. This isn't abstract. If you don't know someone, it's likely only because the someone you do know hasn't told you. It's a private thing, after all.

'Pro-choice' is not a scary term. It doesn't mean 'pro-abortion'. You can be vehemently morally opposed to abortion yourself, but believe in another person's right to autonomy over their body and to determine their own well-being and future. It's supporting someone else's right to choose, not what they choose.

Outlawing abortion doesn't stop it happening. Desperate people will do desperate things in a crisis. Most people don't really want people to harm themselves or be forced into a situation with which they can't cope. Forced pregnancy is classed as torture. Most people aren't for that. The current situation simply places the most hardship on those who can't travel. I believe Ireland is fairer than that.

Gestational limits arguments become another rabbit hole. **It's important people know that ninety per cent of abortions happen in the first twelve weeks,** as soon as someone realises they are pregnant and aren't able to continue, for whatever reason. If the abortion pill were legal here, people could simply take it under their doctor's supervision. **That would be the vast majority of cases.** After that time, you are almost always looking at a wanted pregnancy gone tragically wrong. Imagine putting grieving parents through legal hoops at a time like that? That is why we ask for broader limits.

Remind people that **the Eighth Amendment affects every pregnancy in Ireland. Even a wanted one, even one that you wish to continue.** I'm not sure why we're not more angered about the 'other A' – **Autonomy** – maybe this is an example of how effective anti-choice rhetoric can be. By only focusing on abortion, which they oppose in all cases, we can forget the simple fact that someone can lay hands on or cut us, prescribe or deny us treatment regardless of our wishes, as soon as we're pregnant, because of the Eighth Amendment.

Exceptional cases are called exceptions for a reason. It goes without saying, these need urgent attention from our legislators. But focusing only on them is not a 'middle ground', an unscary way to approach this discussion. In fact, it's dangerous. When you peel back the (undoubtedly) good intentions, you find a pretty misogynistic stance. **If you're okay with abortion in the case of rape, incest and fatal foetal abnormality, you're okay with abortion, just not with how a person gets pregnant.** You, in fact, are the one playing judge and jury on which pregnancies it's all right to end, so long as the pregnant person has suffered. It's hard to put this concept gently, because it deeply challenges a stance many are proffering as a moderate way. But it needs to be challenged. It would see little change and might, in fact, allow our government to claim action and return to deafness on this issue. We can't leave the majority behind.

There is no Repeal or reproductive rights movement without you. Join a group, or don't. March, or wear a badge. Have a chat. Write to your TD. It's all going to count. There is no Repeal movement to point to, because it's you too. **If you hear anyone saying 'Repeal the Eighth should …' ask them who they mean.** If they're pro-repeal, ask them what they're doing themselves. If they're not, let their words wash over you. They're just words.

Hopefully they'll get on board soon and do something, because we need all hands on deck. This will be driven by all of us, with all our different backgrounds: social, political – some of us are even from Cork. Don't tell us we're doing it wrong, do something yourself. We have enough obstacles and we're doing our best with nothing. Thank you.

Lastly, here's my Safe Cross Code for talking about repro rights.

STOP. Don't knee-jerk. All we've ever heard about this issue until recently has come from one side. Some of the things you've heard about abortion might not be true. There are people with good intentions spreading myths about it; but be aware there are others more cynically actively twisting truth and attempting to discredit those they disagree with. Educate yourself as best you can. Spread the word.

LOOK at who you're talking to. Assess whether the conversation is worth both your energies. Be gentle if the person is coming from lived experience – talking likely takes it out of them. If the person is vehemently opposed, let them off. That's their belief. But do remind them that **we're not asking them to change their minds, just to be allowed to make up our own.**

LISTEN to **experts.** Not people who simply don't agree. This isn't some abstract concept for debate. Instead, listen to people who have researched and thought about this in real terms, or are coming from a legal, human rights or medical background. I recommend the Abortion Rights Campaign, Amnesty International, The Coalition to Repeal the Eighth Amendment and organisations like Doctors for Choice and Lawyers for Choice (who can tell you all about legislation post-repeal), TFMR, Parents for Choice and AIMS Ireland (particularly on consent during continued pregnancy). The real, impartial information is out there. Make it your mission to seek it out and share it.

There's a lot to be done, but I know that, together, we can do it. Please, don't let negative chatter put you off. Please, keep talking. Repeal the Eighth.

TROLLING THE WEB

55

TO BE FRANK

A fictitious response to some very real messages received on social media.

10 December

Frank couldn't sleep. Again. Exhausted, he pulled on his raincoat and shut the door behind him as quietly as he could. He'd have loved to have slammed it. Might have made him feel better. Feel something other than rage. But he didn't want to risk waking his ma.

Sucking hard on one of the rollies he'd spent the earlier part of the evening preparing, he paced the glistening streets nearby (she didn't like him to go too far) to try to still his racing mind. There was so much to be angry about. So much injustice, against him. He leaned against the underside of a railway bridge to contemplate this. A young woman passed. He thought about following her. Not to do anything, he didn't think. His presence alone would be enough to unsettle her – it was after midnight and there was no one else around. Even the Spar was shut. His ma called his raincoat his 'flasher mac' but, now he thought about it, he wasn't about to share his mighty sword with some bitch stupid enough to walk home on her own. You never know who you might meet under a railway bridge. *Stupid bitch.* Look at her, looking back, taking him in. Getting her keys out of her bag. Scared. *Good.* His pulse raced. He should get home. In bed he gave himself a gentle tug of justice while trawling random Facebook profiles and fell asleep with his laptop on his chest.

11 December

Frank's ma woke him, as usual, with a cup of tea in bed before she left for work. He would have liked to sleep on a bit, but, not wanting to disappoint her, he sat up, sipped and wished her a lovely day. He reached across the covers for his laptop as he heard the door snap shut behind her. Something was eating at him. He was only half awake, but something was eating him, up and down, inside and out. Some old bint. Some old bint he'd crept past on his bedtime trawl. Someone he'd kind of heard of, but not really. Her face. *Her fucking face.* What was her name again? Didn't matter. He hit 'back' until he found her. God, she annoyed him. And she was old – the 'old' part really irked him. A long, empty day was stretching out ahead. He lit one of last night's rollies and started a message. A message of release, of *justice.* He wrote to the old bint, not just for himself, but for all mankind:

09.44 *Why can't you be prettier, and funnier?*

Yeah. She called herself a comedian. But women aren't funny – with their period jokes and … that's it. That would show her. He felt himself get hard.

Minutes passed and Frank was flaccid again. She hadn't responded. *Cheeky bitch.* Sword in hand, he slashed through her profile, looking for – and finding! – fuel for his rage. *Cats.* She'd fostered cats for some fucking cat charity, the lonely old spinster. If this were medieval times, she'd have been burnt at the stake by now.

10.19 *You sad old cunt, with your cats!*

Hahahaha! This was great. But it wasn't enough. Time to go back to how she looked. Go in harder.

10.27 *Judging by your identical forced grin, I would say you are deeply unhappy and lonely.*

Identical to what, he didn't say, but it didn't matter. That wasn't Frank's point. He didn't have to tell her: who was she, his ma? Now all he had to do was wait.

And wait.

Christmas. New Year. Nothing. No reply – it looked like she hadn't even read them. But he saw this old bitch with her lonely forced identical grin cropping up on telly now and again, talking about some book she'd written.

12 February

Who the fuck did she think she was, the past-it old crone? Did she think she was pretty enough to be on telly? To not even reply to his messages? To ignore him and his mighty sword? *The state of her.* He was supposed to be going out for a pint – he could do that on a Monday, he liked having the pub to himself – but, all these months later, he had to get this burning off his chest and the roaring out of his head.

18:45 *Did you take your Prozac today, you dried up old cunt?*

Depression and menopause in one go. Genius! He should be a writer himself. Why did this witch have a book? Was the stupid thing selling, anyway? Where would he even check? He wasn't sure and there was no time. You're a writer, Frank. Make something up.

18:57 *Heading towards 400 copies of your epic sold; will a Pulitzer make up for the lack of husband?*

Frankie boy, you're on fire! He didn't know what a Pulitzer was, really, or if she had a husband, he hadn't read her profile properly. He'd been so blinded by cats. Which reminded him …

20:37 *HRT plus cat equals evolutionary dead end*

It wasn't even English but, already mid tug, Frank was past caring. The *coup de grâce*. He'd called her out on being childless. A woman of her age. This was as close to a stake as you could legally get these days, *more's the pity*. For a brief, post-tug moment, he felt good. What a day! What a time to be alive!

Before heading out to the pub, Frank kissed his ma on the cheek and told her he wouldn't be late.

56

ACCESS ALL AREAS

It's my fault. I've been misleading. I love to chat and engage online as far as is reasonable, but it seems I've blurred the lines. So let me take responsibility and put it right by saying this: we don't know each other.

I know! Mad, isn't it? We don't really know anyone we only know online or, if they're even a vaguely public figure, from their work. Even though social media has brought us all together and the world's really peaceful and harmonious right now. (Not. Weird that constant chatter and being able to message Kim and Kanye doesn't seem to be deepening understanding.)

We can see what Kimye had for breakfast, because they show it to us. But we don't know what they truly thought of it, or if they even ate it. I thought we knew this? Fourteen-year-olds do. What we share online isn't the whole story.

In my own case, I try to be the same person on social media as off it, but I like to think that while I'm an idiot, I'm not a *total* idiot: there's plenty I don't share. Selfies of me crying, how I vote, dishes mounting in the sink, the majority of my swears. But the second something's public (sadly everyone's life is a bit public now, even those who haven't chosen public lives) someone will complete the jigsaw with their own imagined pieces. The picture's distorted.

Humour's not only part of my job; it's my pressure valve. It makes me happy. I only speak seriously when I feel there really is no other option: I'm no political analyst, or therapist, or expert of any kind. I'm often self-wrong-teous. Debating leaves me cold. It never really solves anything and at its worst ends up being two sides attempting unsuccessfully to have an intellectual wank at each other. Personally, I only enjoy physical ones, as you know. (More on that in the final chapter.) Take a debate online and it can become even more pointless. So I don't do it.

There's a certain kind of person I encounter, almost never someone I actually know. Let's call them Mr/Ms/Mx Persistent. They want engagement and they want it now and they want the kind they want – as if people are commentary ATMs or online room service. And Mr/Ms/Mx Persistent doesn't even tip.

In the course of the interaction, they expertly manage to erase you or me – the human at the other end – and not take a polite no for an answer. Maybe I don't want to play today? Or ever? Maybe I've said all I have to say on a topic? Maybe my status update wasn't actually an opening? Maybe I'm on the phone to my mum about Dad's gravestone at the moment? Maybe I've been working away and haven't seen my husband in a week? But no, they want a response *now*. They somehow believe it's my duty.

clears throat

It's not.

I see online interaction like going to someone's real-life home: the door may be open, but it's still nice to knock. Their having a toilet somewhere, or endorsing the concept of toilets, doesn't entitle you to take a shit in the hallway. Please leave when they start looking at their watches and doing fake yawns. They kindly let you in – they shouldn't need a bouncer to show you out. We've all had enough of Shitness and there are only small corners of our world we can protect from it. Let's ask for it. It's time to demand more real-life courtesy, better boundaries from internet behaviour, just like we would in real life.

Like I said at the start, all of this is just my opinion, here to take or leave and hopefully entertain; I'm afraid I can't come over to dissect it. I'll chat about it, definitely, but back and forth in essay form? No thank you. What Mr/Ms/Mx Persistent seems to be looking for from me isn't on offer.

They argue that 'it's public'. Yes, so is my doorstep and I'm still entitled to personal boundaries once I cross it. Just because I say something I'm happy to stand over doesn't automatically make it an invitation to go over it again, all day long, with people I don't know. At least therapists get paid. And if you pushed like that for engagement in offline real life – the pub, say – at least one of us would be perfectly entitled to drink up and leave if they weren't in the mood.

What I expect from the internet is cat videos, to be honest. I use it for work, but the best thing about it is cat videos. Those I will chat about all day long.

There is, at least, a certain honesty to trolls. They swoop in, are shitty and are easily blocked. But the Persistent often Trojan in softly, almost sweetly, and without warning you realise you're in a correspondence to rival St Paul and the Corinthians, for which you didn't sign up. That's why the 140 characters on Twitter were my favourite. (Please don't change it, please. Oh, they have.) In longer forms, people can more quickly assume a familiarity that doesn't really exist and then overstep.

Public faces are edited highlights. People who seem sorted are usually not, same as the rest of us. So, sometimes, I mind myself and say, 'I'm not discussing this today.' And suddenly I'm 'silencing'. 'Book burning.' 'Selfish!'

'I only wanted to chat,' they'll say. Well, all I'm saying is I may not be free or able to play the way you want today, Mr/Ms/Mx Persistent. You didn't elect me. You don't pay for that service. We don't even know each other. And I need some time to watch cat videos. End of discussion.

57

TO FEED OR NOT TO FEED THE TROLLS

While I'm a massive fan of social media and spent large chunks of 2009 urging pals to join Twitter, there isn't a single kind of troll that hasn't visited me. Obviously, I'm in no way unique; they tend to do the rounds, like the neighbours at Christmas. And I'm definitely not the first to write about this, but I feel the need.

When I say 'troll' I'm not talking about those with whom I have simple disagreements; as you saw in the last chapter, I think back and forths on social media are futile, and sometimes it's okay to say, 'I've said all I have to say' or even 'I've said all I have to say *to you*.' I'm referring to those out to insult, derail, silence or plain old needle. The ones I end up blocking. The ones who – when you check their timelines – have been blocked by others and proclaim 'Blocked by X! Typical. They can't handle my truth!' No, mate: they can't handle the boredom incurred by your intrusive nonsense. And therein lies the biggest – and possibly most surprising – problem with being trolled. It's. So. BORING.

They'll swoop in and say something personal. Or send abhorrent pictures. Or debunked facts. Or, my favourite: whataboutery. 'You're talking about X, why not about Y?' Well, 'cos I'm not. Mentioning the effects of the Eighth Amendment or racist abuse or whatever on me or someone close to me doesn't mean I don't care about homelessness, depression, suicide rates etc., etc., etc., but sheesh – the pieces would be fierce long if I had to mention *all of the things*. Naively, I used to waste time trying to get whatabouterers to see that I did care about *all of the things!* Not any more. I now see it for the derailing attempt that it is. 'Feminists are terrible, pretending there's no domestic violence against men.' That sort of thing. As I once learned with a lame International Men's Day joke, where I stupidly wished everyone twenty-four hours of being treated the same as women are (shudder), these lads aren't out to raise awareness of male suicide, depression or domestic violence against men, which is a shame. Instead they're out to use it to say, 'Shut up about feminism/racism/whatever. It doesn't affect me and I'm tired of it.' Well, my dear online non-friend, maybe I'm getting a little tired of you.

They may not be as extreme as those very special troll people, like the ones who targeted *Ghostbusters/SNL* actor Leslie Jones, but that doesn't absolve them of trollery. They often don't see themselves as abusive, but their repeated (and repeated and repeated) insistence tips them over into Blockland. Recently, after one of these columns, someone kept on asking why I didn't talk about ISIS and condemn their actions against women. All day. Even though it had nothing to do with that day's piece, I was with family and my Middle Eastern politics expertise is zero. But they wouldn't stop. I said, 'That's interesting, but I'm not getting into it,' maybe five times before deciding to mute. Even if well-intentioned and informed, that 'No. Answer me!' stuff drags that person dangerously close to under-bridge living.

Everyone has their own way of dealing with trolls. Actually, everyone *thinks* they have a way of dealing with them, a pre-ordained strategy for when they come knocking and just won't leave. *Don't feed them. Give them zero cake and they'll soon be on their way.* But not everyone has reason to test it. No one size fits all, if you've ever been the target of a swarm, or there are threats. Then, simply ignoring them can feel like they've won. You take it and take it, not responding. Let me tell you, this so-called high road is pretty lonely and doesn't always feel very good.

My husband has had a lifetime of race-related abuse, some of it physical. For example, when he goes home to Los Angeles, I beg him to stay safe. He knows what I mean and if he's pulled over for even the most minor traffic violation, he starts recording on his phone. On the back of all this abuse he has taught me a rule: if someone aggresses you, while it might not be good or smart to punch back, pushing back is vital. You need to let them know you're not their free punchbag. If you want to retweet abuse, let other people know you're being aggressed, that's okay too. It's not encouraging a pile-on – they started the abuse and you want help. To paraphrase Lindy West (who's written brilliantly on the topic following some of the worst trolling imaginable), do whatever makes you feel better in the face of someone trying to make you feel bad.

People mean well when they give the stock counsel: *Ignore! Be better!* But when dealing with repeated personal abuse that goes deeper than the usual (and expected) *You're an awful eejit* or *You're not funny*, or *You're ugly* (#bantz), it's not always possible to turn the other cheek. Nor is it necessarily best. Depriving them of the oxygen of attention can come later; you forget they exist as soon as they no longer have access. In the pre-blocking moment, though, I'm with West: sometimes it's best to respond – preferably in burn form – before you report.

My current strategy? Two responses, then block. And a lot of mute. So much mute.

The internet's an awful lot more fun that way. Taking out the trash really gives the old place a lift.

Update:
Did I get trolled when this column went live? You better believe it!
#boring #predictable #yawn #mute #next

58

HOW DO YOU SLEEP?

I've had a lot of sleepless nights of late, much of it Shitness-related, during which I try not to lie there, attributing terrifying personae to the ceiling shadows. I might try to read some fiction – if I can do it without waking the fella. (I'm a pretty noisy reader.) I might sneak downstairs and watch something trashy (duh); something in which people in expensive outfits fight about who sits next to whom at a gala (pronounced *gayla* or *galla* with way too much *ahhh*). I might stay in bed and focus on my breathing, but then I realise it's shallow and horrified and it just wakes me right up again. I might listen to music. They say it soothes the savage, horrified breast.

What I really try to avoid is thinking. I get enough of that during the day.

During waking hours, with the world casually sliding hell-wards, I'm doing whatever I need to do to facilitate sleep later. Have I done enough? Said enough? Even though only I know what my getting to sleep is going to take, some people tell me I'm doing it wrong. Hear that? I'm even doing insomnia wrong, say self-appointed experts. This makes me want to go round to their house at 3 a.m. with an old-fashioned metal dustbin and a loud and mangy cat and serenade them with 'Un Bel Di Vedremo' from *Madame Butterfly* while kicking the bin and swinging the cat around my head. If you think *that's* cruel, I'm not even a soprano! The whole thing would be a crime. But it'd make me feel better.

I am so sick of being 'splained at. I get 'splained at all day long these days. The internet lets them all in: strangers, Muddeners, well-meaning friends – people with ideas that as we know are only ideas, opinions, counselling those who actually have to live with something daily. At best, we have a great discussion. At worst, they gaslight – say my setting them straight on any abuse I receive is shutting down discussion. But I don't have the power to shut anything down. I wish I did, I'd get a lot more sleep. What they really seem to mean is 'Shh, little lady. Let me do the thinking 'round here. I have this perception of a thing I haven't experienced but because it's in my head, it's right. No, no, no – I don't want to hear about what it means in the real world! It's in ma head, sweetheart. Ma head. Maaaa heeeaaddd.'

So, let's agree to disagree! Why not? Disagreement's great, especially when you agree to do it. But that's not what they want, not really. What they want is to put me in my place. They want me to shut up. They might not have Pepe the (unintentionally) Nazi frog for an avatar, but nor do they feel like examining or unpicking the position you've taken, so they'll switch it, say I'm presuming moral superiority. I'm preaching. The irony. Young Pepe, it's only my Twitter page. Unfollow. Mute. Ta-da! There ya go! I'm gone! Like magic! Now maybe you'll be able to sleep too.

The world's always been filled with hate and the need of one group to control another, so the super-fast change of late is really a super-fast revealing of old fear and insecurity that's newly found direction, targets and a chilling social acceptability. Decency – the real kind, not some imagined, nostalgic version – has been supplanted by a need to hear all 'sides' when one side barely conceals the wish to remove the rights of the other. Let them speak in your own house if you must. I've already heard them. They've been clear. Their wishes are known. I don't need to hear them again. I'd like to be able to sleep.

As a weird, intense teenager, I loved classical music. I don't think I told many people. I'm sure I said I loved The Beatles and Bowie, which was also 100 per cent true, but loving classical music wasn't cool. I did, though. I loved it. I used to get opera records from Cork City library and probably cry for the whole two weeks I'd have them because you can't beat the combination of incredible voices and raging hormones. I've recently been drawn back to this kind of music. I need to soothe my soul.

I can't take any more hot takes from people not affected one jot by what they're discussing. I can't take people who call women Feminazis while defending *actual* Nazis. I can't take fake news being hurled at the world like urine onto a hotel sheet, so we're distracted from real harm being done. I can't take intellectual shapes being thrown by those with gaps in their awareness, gaps they have no interest in bridging. I can't take the lack of kindness.

I always thought the reason it was mainly older people who seemed drawn to classical music was because they had mellowed. But now I'm getting on myself, I realise the opposite is true. The sorrow for the world. The rage. It just keeps coming. And you burn, not mellow at all. You need something beautiful, soaring, to lift you. Something to drown out the incessant bile and, in many ways worse than the bile itself, those telling you you should be letting it in.

Nah, mate. I've got a date with Puccini. Piss off.

59

TIME FOR A SPRING CLEAN, DICK PICS AND ALL

Intermission –
Yikes, things have gotten heavy again. Let's lighten them with some penises, yeah?

I love it when it's official. When you can call it. Spring, I mean. When the sun's no longer all slanty-ways and dazzling; instead it seems to land directly on surfaces and bathe them in beautiful, unhelpful golden tones so you can't but see it. *It.* Dirt, dust, the unmistakeable air of neglect. Last week it was invisible. Now it's everywhere. Face it, you're no dusting dervish either. You haven't had to be. It's all been a trick of the light.

What's with those smears on the window? Who smeared them? The dog can't be responsible for fingerprints, can he? (If he is, we might have greater problems on our hands.) I hadn't realised that the non-human cast of *Arachnophobia* had not only set up camp in the flat, but staged a full Spidey Mardi Gras. Cobweb streamers everywhere. And the dust. The dust. Not a fine sprinkle, like a detective might use to ascertain if it really was the dog at the window, but what can only be described as a drift. You could ski down the piles of it, is what I'm saying.

But no one can judge us because we didn't know! It's the light's fault, shining in, making us all aware. Even filtered as it is through smears, springy brightness reveals things I'd rather not acknowledge about my cleaning skills, which I had up until then thought were all right. Not amazing but, you know, I have a feather duster. I don't know where it is, but I do have one. It's probably under the stairs with all the other things I don't want to think about, but I don't want to think about that now.

This reminds me of the Facebook spring cleans people do; those vaguely threatening culls that are announced every now and again, like a decree from the castle steps. 'If you're seeing this now, you have survived. You are chosen. This means your status updates mostly don't make me want to tear my own face off.' We've all wanted to tear our own faces off when reading other people's status updates – I tore mine off only yesterday – but … isn't it sort of wanky to say it? I spend much of my time on social media assuming that someone is tearing their own face off out of frustration or boredom or agreement with me. I encourage them to mute: sure, I've got nothing. Such cull threats, I feel, merely state the obvious, aggressively.

Then there's the self-appointed Social Media Sanitation Department (SMSD), who sigh and eye roll their way through the internet, bemoaning the way everyone uses it but them. Perched high on their online-street-sweeper yokes, they denounce others' insincerity and accuse them of grief-trolling when a celebrity dies. 2016 was a busy time for them. They eye-roll, that is, until somebody *they* admire dies. Then it's all inspirational quotes and videos and everyone should back off because this time the grief – their grief – is authentic.

As for the lads who send unsolicited dick pics … Oh lads, I know where I'd like to put my feather duster, if I could find it. Penises are fine in and of themselves. Great, in fact. But an unsolicited lad is a little much before noon. And the prelude is the real sickener; it's so widespread, I'm starting to wonder if they teach it in schools. The prelude? You know it. Ah, you do. It goes like this:

'Hi cutie. What's your name?'

It's on my profile. Maybe read it?

'Haha. You're a sassy one.'

I don't use FB for this kind of exchange. Goodbye.

'Why, cutie? What are you afraid of?'

That my dog has developed opposable thumbs and is using them to smear the windows and buy treats on eBay. So, bye now. BTW please don't send me a di... Ah, too late, there it is.

Far more honest, surely, to just send the dick pic? I mean, it's still rude, but why beat about the proverbial and waste all those letters you obviously hate?

These days 'Hey babys', spam about decking, and/or unsolicited dicks (I'm not sure that's the best way to sell decks) all go the way of my block button. No fanfare, no decree from the steps.

Like many actors and comedians who aren't mega famous, I used to use my personal Facebook page for work. I've had to separate them now. If Twitter is bad for people over-stepping the mark, Facebook is like people getting into bed with you and stealing all the covers. So I've reluctantly had to make two pages: a small public page for anyone who wants public Tara Flynn news, and a private page with a fake name and non-specific photo. Lads, the dicks dried up overnight. It's the best thing I ever did. I still have to let people know about what I'm up to, though I swear when I'm a multimillionaire and have my own publicist, that private page will just be pictures of my dog and sandwiches (which, for all I know, he may have made himself, using his secret thumbs). Anyway, it'll definitely make you want to tear your face off. Till then, I will have to engage in shameless plugging on both pages (which the SMSD are of course on like a shot), though I no longer accept the friend requests of people I don't know well. I had let too many strangers in. It was my own fault, but boy did it open a can of worms. And by worms, of course I mean penises. Where are the SMSD then, huh? Where? Not on worm patrol, that's for sure.

Despite the protestations of the SMSD about how overworked they and their rolling eyes are, this can't be new. I'm sure wealthy Victorian scoundrels had portrait artists round to render their lad in oils and then deliver the resulting dick-canvas to the homes of random women. At least nowadays you can block or delete dick pics. It must have been horrific to have to keep them in the attic.

60

FREEZEPEACH

A potential girlfriend for Frank from 'To Be Frank'. A 'guy's girl'. Not one of those shrill Feminazis.

I'm Freezepeach99. I'm a Cool Girl. I do everything I can think of that boys are supposed to like. And guess what? Boys do like me. I'm not shrill or boring or threatening. I'm cool.

I haven't eaten bread since the 1990s. My shape must be precise. My hair is straightened out. Polite, demure. But sassy, on my own terms.

I'm funny, but not in your face. I try hard not to try hard. I have a neat line in approving giggles. Sometimes you need to reflect coolness back onto others. Sometimes, it's better to do that than to shine. Sometimes, you just need to be a cool mirror.

When I have time, I write about how straight, white men are the only truly oppressed group in the world, and how political correctness is the real enemy. Because it is. It's humourless. Irrational. I'm one of the lads, y'see. I have to be able to laugh along with them. How can I be an all-rounder if I can't snigger at my own gender? *Hello? Sense of humour?* (Just not too much. I'm capable of deep seriousness too.) I'm open to criticism. Debate. Criticism. That's how we learn. Can you prove women don't have smaller brains? So what if we do? I mean, how else would they fit in our smaller heads? How would we be able to wear so many different kinds of hat?

Feminism is for old, washed-up women who wouldn't know *huevos rancheros* if they came up and bit them at brunch. So, I love to throw the cat among their pigeons. I'm nothing if not a delightful contradiction. Shopping isn't cool any more? It's a blatant display of materialism? Well, check out my new Victoria's Secret haul. It's so heavy it's pulling my shoulder out of my socket, but I'm worth it.

I am completely bare *down there*. (I don't like the V-word; it's vulgar.) It's like that one time this guy told me he was disgusted because I wasn't properly groomed and I had no option but to agree with him. I was disgusting. Now I never go more than a couple of weeks without visiting my waxer. Wax on, wax off, done. It hardly hurts at all any more. It's worth it not to be disgusting.

I hate women comedians. They're ugly, that's why they have to try so hard. I'm pretty funny, like I said, but with me, it's effortless. I don't show off, that's what's great about me. The trick is to disguise when you're performing. It gives you more allure.

What's wrong with making a guy feel special, more secure? Doesn't everyone want to make their partner feel good? I don't know how those *capital-eff all-caps FEMINISTS* get on with their men, if any of them have real men at all. Their 'fellas' are presumably hen-pecked and brow-beaten like the pussies they are. They need to grow some balls and take those humourless wenches in hand. I don't know many women who'd put up with these women either.

I am not a homophobe. But you don't see me walking up to you to tell you I'm straight, do you?

I have my own job. I use contraception. I vote. But I'm not a feminist because no one tells me what to do. I'm no sheep. And I'm strategic about what really works in this world. Quotas don't: the best man for the job might be edged out *because women*. That's just fucked up.

I will say one thing to your face, as my mascara streams down it in a nightclub; I will say another when I'm performing for *them*. The lads. So authentic.

You don't have to go on protests all the time. What do you want for it? A medal? You're scaring people. Keep your voices down. We're all equal, we get it, but you're putting people off. No wonder they say women are too mouthy and too much. I agree.

Free speech means hearing out my opinions. Don't like them? Well, *you need to understand that you don't understand* the intellectual thrust of rational thought.

Racist? Sexist? Challenging thoughts too big for your small brains, more like: I only understand because I stay just quiet enough to learn. If we constantly silence harmful, unpopular thoughts, bad people will only be driven further down the roads of the thinking you call bad. You will have caused the harm. *You.* You just don't get it, do you?

Maybe guys would treat you nicer if you wore a better bra? Some nice lipstick, maybe? Maybe you just need to be more pleasant.

He didn't mean it, it was just a joke. Not that one, that wasn't a joke, lighten up for fuck's sake.

I laugh about you, with them. We think you're fools. We see why you're behind. We see why you're less. We know why we … We … I … We …

I'm a man's woman, ya know? I swear like a trooper. One of the guys.

I don't hate women, some of my best friends are …

Women are the ones I call at night when I can't sleep. I'm there for my girls, but let's keep it light.

I'm into rap and death metal and his poems. So deep and dark. You could swim in them if you were brave enough. His words are fire. You wouldn't understand.

Freezepeach. Free speech. Haha! In-joke. I think he made it up.

He reminds me daily that James Connolly died for my coffee break. I am forever grateful for the reminder.

I wait for you to have a bad day. And then I'm on you. I slide into DMs, I sneer, I am on the front line now.

You think you're better than him? He's a free speech hero, don't shut him down. Don't you ignore him. Hey, hey you, hey, HEY, hey! Answer him! Did you mute him, you coward? Would you have run away as quick in 1916?

Don't get your knickers in a twist, sweetheart. Where did you get them, by the way? You deserve better. He deserves to be driven wild by desire, by you. Why don't you let him have that? You should love yourself more. You should be cool.

I am. I am cool. I am one of the lads, and I'm cool.

THE BIZ

61

HOMESICK

I'm homesick! I'm not too far from home as I write this, only in London, but I am. I know I'm not eight and that my work means I'll always have to go where the job is (*Who doesn't?* says you), but it doesn't make missing home any easier.

I'm not quite at the stage where I cry at the mere sound of an uilleann pipe warming up, but have I sussed which shops stock Irish papers? Hell, yeah. And I've realised something. For all its flaws, I've fallen back in love with Ireland. In 2006 I moved to London, not sure I'd ever go home. When I did move back in 2011, it was more to do with circumstance than choice. I loved London, I'd made a life here for five years, met my husband and got married, done work I was proud of and I was very sad to leave my friends. But the truth is, Ireland's great again. I'm not talking about the 'green shoots recovery' bullshit spouted by those in government: you can only walk past so many sleeping bags on the most affluent of streets without seeing that for the horseshit it is. You know they're talking donkey crap when your mum spends a night on a trolley in A&E. But, so long as we don't lose the run of ourselves when they tell us to this time, Ireland's an exciting place to be.

I don't have my finger on the pulse by any means; when I kick off my shoes, it's more likely to be sofa-bound than dance floor-adjacent. But even I can smell the potential, bubbling away. Irish people are making such exciting work again. And they're making it out of nothing, like artsy magicians. I'm not happy there isn't more remuneration for them; in reality, they should be paid more for the expertise of getting an idea (a book, a blog, a poem, a song, a short film, club night, café, game, piece of visual or street art, furniture, you name it) to happen with practically no resources other than imagination and hard work. The arts and showbiz are a 'Biz', after all. More often than not we have to rely on mates willing to help make ideas happen. But those mates seem to be back in abundance. Fewer people seem to be asking 'What's in it for me?' than they were when I fell out of love with us a bit. Instead, they seem to want to help something take shape. Live music's exciting again, theatre's taking chances and Irish writers, film-makers, artists and scientists are world-renowned. Most are not benefitting financially much, if at all, but that's not stopping them making like maniacs. People seem kinder, more supportive than when they were running around buying flats for the craic. This, here, is a boom worth getting excited about.

When I first moved back from London, I was so worried about 'the economy' (which was all I was hearing our politicians talk about on the radio) that I brought an American husband back with me to try to help boost it. Surely he'd buy souvenirs and pay entry fees into touristy castles? I didn't even get a prize for this hands-on helping, and I should have realised what was to come as soon as I saw that the Taoiseach wasn't at the ferry port to meet us. Though, admittedly, the American didn't end up buying as many Aran jumpers as I'd thought he might.

And now I'm back in London for a bit. I shouldn't be homesick at all: I'm doing an Irish play (*All That Fall*), by an Irish writer (Samuel Beckett, he's good), with an Irish cast. I practically haven't left. But it's definitely London. Glenn Close is only working around the corner, for feck's sake. It's one of the greatest cities in the world, of which I have many brilliant memories, and it's lovely to be back. Then there's the architecture! The galleries! The West

End shows (if you can afford them)! The people! The Tube! The parks in the sun!

I'm living out of a suitcase and prevailing on the hospitality of some beyond-generous pals but that's not what has me missing the old sod. True, I can't leave my socks lying around or my towel on the floor, even for a minute, even if I'm 'coming right back to it'. That would be rude. Having to be tidy is a downer for me. My local, well, isn't local now, it's miles away. Home is where the heart is. My fella. My pets. My sofa (I really do love being on it).

Nice to realise, though, that it's not just them I'm pining for. That despite all the brilliant things London has to offer, it turns out I'm living in the right country right now. Nice to realise Ireland's home again.

At the very start of *All That Fall*, Beckett makes sure you know where we're headed by having Christy's hinny do a big donkey/horse crap which Christy offers to sell to Maddy as dung. Luckily, in Ireland today, we don't have to accept manure, even when they try to sell it to us. They won't fool us this time. We're no donkeys.

62

WORK OF ART

When I told my parents I wanted to act, they suggested I go for a good long walk for myself. In the country, a good long walk was the cure for all ills, including bad ideas. 'Why not teach? Your grandmother was a teacher,' they'd say, or spell out in golden syrup on my porridge. Or 'Why not look for a job in Brussels with that French of yours?'

The fear of God was in them. Dad had wanted to be an actor; he had taken some classes and done lots of 'am dram' ('like Richard Harris'). He'd planned to move to Dublin after school, even though one of the Abbey Players had replied to a letter he'd sent, responding with something like, 'Of course be an actor, if you fancy starving in a garret for the rest of your life.' He was undeterred. But then his mother died of cancer, far too young, and his father needed help supporting the family. So Dad got a 'real' job. He knew first-hand how, in life, we can't always do what we feel called to do. We definitely can't do it and expect security.

But that doesn't mean that the Arts aren't real and serious work. You have to stay motivated, even knowing that you may never get that break; you may be poor for the rest of your life. Most artists juggle the art part of their lives around bill-paying jobs, admin, kids.

When people dismiss the Arts as airy, flighty nonsense, it doesn't fit with the hardworking creative people I know. I remember meeting someone who'd retrained as an actor in his thirties, because 'he hated getting up early'. I laughed for hours. Hauling ass to a cold rehearsal room while it's still dark, having to be mentally and physically alert, was a literal eye-opener for him. Filming (should you be so lucky) almost always manages to mean a dawn call – and then you might not get used for hours. Artists have cold hands; who are these kings who can afford a heated workspace?

We are delighted to be working at all. We might bitch about deadlines, or a difficult, exhausting rehearsal process, but they also thrill us; they mean there's a job, maybe even some pay. (It is the Biz, after all.) But where the craft lies, what people who might not work in the arts forget to value, is the work no one sees. The binned drafts. The recycled clay, the choreography that doesn't click. It's heartbreaking and nobody knows or cares; why should they? Except that that is where the real work is. That's where experience blossoms. The sheer doing it everyday is the 'genius', not the flash of inspiration that can lead to acclaim. Not the jammy gig, the big commission, the showy role.

I write about remuneration for art (and the scam of paying with 'exposure') elsewhere, so I won't dwell on it here. Because the point here is vocation. Art has to be a vocation or it simply wouldn't be worth your while. You'd give up. It's often thankless. Full of rejection. It's hard. But then sometimes, just sometimes, there's something greater than financial reward or recognition; the expression of something that desperately needs to come out. Maybe even a purging of poison. Giving others the means to, and opportunity for, some urgent conversation.

There was an excellent spoken word festival in Dublin, Lingo Festival, and I was lucky enough to be part of a panel called 'Kick Up The Arts'. We discussed art's place in social change. I wrote a piece for it. I'm going to leave you with a bit of it:

Art bursts out.

   When no one will listen. When you can contain it no longer. Art bursts out, instead of sending up a flare. Instead of setting things on fire. So you don't hurt someone else the way you're hurting.

It's a scream.

It's an ideal to strive for.

It's an expression we can wear on our bodies, paint on walls, sing at the top of our lungs.

Art makes things digestible, even if it causes indigestion first. It doesn't have to be pastoral, it should not be pleasant and we've always known that in this country.

Art is the way in to the discussions governments won't have. We know that it's important when it draws the hatred out, shines light on dark corners where hate lives and hides and snipes. Some threaten us with harm – even shallow graves – for words we've written, filmed or sung. We do not realise our power till then. They do. They see our power. So we should use it. Hard.

We remember that Art bursts out best from attempts to silence us. The time for the podium has passed: Irish women are sending up flares. We hope someone will see them, from the air.

Our work can live and breathe and scream. Can help to ease our pain. One day, it might become a document. For now, it is the history, unfolding. They'll see it, when they look back. They'll say they got it, then.

They think Art is decoration, the bit around the edges. They do not know: it is our beating heart. We do not make the work as-well-as; the work bursts out because it can't stay in.

That is a real service. I believe that is of value.

63

DON'T SHOOT: LIGHTS, CAMERA, ANXIETY

As I write, I'm getting ready to have my photo taken. Though it's part of the whole being-an-actor deal, I cannot adequately express how much terror this fills me with. But let me try.

There's a knot in my stomach. My fine lines (the ones I'd love not to catch the carefully positioned lights) crease a little deeper. The advance guard of upper-lip sweat arrives early in the day and will not be tamed by powdering.

Photographers often get cross with me. I'm tense and awkward about having my picture taken, so I usually make their day much harder just by showing up. Plus, I don't have a 'beauty face'. NB: this is NOT fishing for compliments. I'm grand. No, this is what I've learned from years around cameras and comments. I'm okay about it. I have other strengths. Photographers are often used to working with modelly wans: tall, gorgeous, aware of all their angles – not one of which is bad. When I arrive, there's a lot of busy moving of reflectors, lots of getting me to turn my head till it's almost out of shot (which, believe me, makes me much more comfortable). Then, my heart sinking, they try to get me to do Klassic Komedy Shotz: things that make me want to vom when I see other people doing them and now they want other people to vom when they see me. Things like jumping up in the air with my two legs going opposite ways, or peeping out from behind a potted plant (Zany!), or pretending to be putting my head in the mouth of a plastic tiger (Raar!), or another comedian, if there are no plastic tigers about. They were bad ideas when I was in my twenties and being asked to do them the first time, and, in my humble opinion, they're even worse now. If there's anything that depresses me quicker than wackiness, I don't know what it is. But as God is my witness, I'm a mature(ish) person now: I will never make a wheelbarrow with another comic outside the International Bar or Kilkenny Castle again.

I've no fear of looking silly – if you've seen me on telly, you've seen me in wigs. Put me in character and I'm fine. Roll camera, all day long. Call 'action' and I'll do practically anything. (I said 'practically'.) When I'm thinking about the scene, I'm not really thinking about how I look, which is a lot more fun for me. Stills, where I'm supposed to be just me, reduce me to a quivering mess before I even leave the house.

Leaving the house is a problem all its own: when you're not a big 'sleb with your own team, there are rarely hair and make-up people at the place where the pictures will be taken, so I arrive with half the leaves and debris from the Liffey boardwalk stuck to my electric hair, which is by now a foot taller than when I walked away from my hair straighteners. That's when the supposedly constructive criticisms will start. They will be nice people, lovely shutterbugs, only trying to get a good shot, but they will essentially be pulling at a loose thread that's holding the rest of me together. Before long, I'll have completely unravelled.

'Get your hair out of your eyes!' the photographer will yell. *Jesus, that's my fringe, man!* I can't do without that. It's covering a multitude. I wouldn't advise moving it, but if you do, you'll see: the brows are a nightmare, the brow itself leaves a lot to be desired and CHRIST can you not leave me a bit of structure? The hair's electric, can't you see how it's tall with the static and sticking three feet from my head at the sides? Without the fringe, you may as well send in a picture of a pile of wire wool with nightmare brows. I promise you, I'm saving you a lot of work.

'Do you have a darker lipstick?'

'No.'

The photographer sighs. 'I can't see your lips.'

'What?'

'I can't see your lips.'

'Here they are; where the sound's coming out of.'

'No, they're not reading. They're not reading. How will people know if you've a mouth?'

Then the dreaded: 'Smile more, but open your eyes wide when you do it.'

You don't have to remind me: my face crinkles when I smile, I can't help it. But it's either smile or wide eyes. Not both. If I attempt to do what you've just asked I'll look like something about to be hit by a truck. In fact, I'll look like something that probably should be hit by a truck, to put it out of its misery.

And here's the thing. I don't want to see that picture. I don't want to see 'me' looking tense and feeling inadequate. I'm not a model and I hate that we all seem to have to be, these days. Imperfection is a lost art and I intend to remaster it. Models are lovely and really good at what they do. But I'm also good at what I do, just not so great at what they do. So please, photographers, be gentle. We might not be perfect, but you might like what we have to offer … once you manage to coax us out from behind that hilarious potted plant.

64

MAKING A THING: NOT A FUNNY WORD

My head is so full, it's as if the thoughts and words themselves are pressing on the inside of my skull. My bones and muscles ache. I can't sit still. Even though I'm physically and mentally spent, I'm not sleeping very well. And I've never been happier. You see, I'm making something new.

Making new work is one of the most fun and terrifying things. You can't separate one aspect from the other: without terror, there can be only muted fun. Like a roller coaster. You may be screaming, a little pee may even come out, but the rush makes you feel alive. When it ends, you want to go again.

The anxiety around new work comes in different forms, depending on your job, but we all go through it; a similar feeling to handing in your homework for correction, or presenting an only slightly burnt cake at the end of Home Economics double period. Like, it may not be a perfect cake, but it's your cake. You can't help but hope the teacher doesn't go hard on it. Come on! Only an hour ago there it was, all separate ingredients and no cake. And now there's a cake! The burnt bits? They're your bits! That's what makes it your cake. No better than anyone else's, possibly even objectively worse, but you made that goddamn cake and fair balls. Some people just sit around bitching about cake.

You want it to be good, though. Of course you do. Someone has to eat the cake and you don't wish any one of those prospective tasters any harm. On the contrary, what you picture when you're cracking the eggs into the basin, sieving the flour and praying by an oven door is sheer, cake-induced joy. You want every bite to bring pleasure – or at least to fill a gap: even if your cake is not enjoyed, it should at least fuel someone to their next meal.

But that's not always possible. Not everyone will like your cake.

And here's where some of this week's rush of fear is coming from: I'm putting on new work that's not only new and unproven, it's about something that happened to me. There's no way I can't take the reaction personally. Having worked in comedy for so many years, I'm used to jokes bombing. I'm used to shows getting an audience of three, or to that one audience during the run that seems to have agreed beforehand to sit in angry silence, staring at the holes where the jokes were yesterday (you're sure there were jokes there yesterday). As every performer knows, if things go wrong on stage, you cover it up, you carry on. Because even if the piece is about you, once the thing is up, it's not about you any more. You do your best, make sure what you're saying is clear, but after that, it's about giving people a good night. You have to give your all and, hopefully, their money's worth.

What I've been working on started as a work in progress, as part of the Abbey Theatre's *What's Happening Now* series. Lads, I can't believe it. I've got a brilliant director in Philly McMahon; he's helped me to tease the words all the way from personal testimony to show. It's funny, even though it's about my having to travel to the Netherlands for an abortion. How can something that's not even funny to me be funny to anyone else? Well, that's what I wanted to discover. The public conversation has been dominated by conservative thinkers, with those of us directly affected always having to apologise, or be told that our experience – our real lives – might be unsavoury to some. Well, I've taken my own story back and I'm telling it my way. I hope it demystifies some moments, but mostly, I hope it shows people that each story is unique. There are many facets. Some of them are absurd.

Humour is my own coping mechanism. It's also my job. It's my armour. I didn't lick that off the stones – that's what we do here in Ireland: no matter how dark the subject, we're able to laugh at ourselves. It helps us deal. It helps us heal. But most of all, it makes us real. To remove all humour from a story removes some of its humanity. I may fall flat on my face in my attempt, but telling my own story in my own words is something I had to try.

I'm used to 'jumping off cliffs' on-stage – I've been doing it most Mondays at Dublin Comedy Improv for years. This is different. This might be controversial just because it exists.

But the reason it exists couldn't be further from controversy. In my work is where my story belongs. It's long past time to have some 3D conversations about this topic. There might be some healing laughs along the way. People might even find themselves joining in. I hope.

So, here we go. Roller coaster car teetering at the top.

And … *dive*.

65

THE SHOW MUST GO ON

I'm rarely sick. (Touch wood.) I've been very lucky and in the last twenty or so years, I've only been in hospital as a visitor. But pain comes at ya, fast.

Last week I got a kidney infection. This one was special, because of where it happened – I don't mean where on my body, not beneath my ribs, round the back of my flank, but at the National Theatre. *Amharclann na Mainistreach.* You see, I've only had one kidney infection ever before and I had it when I was doing *I Do Not Like Thee, Doctor Fell* in 2005. Guess where? At the Abbey. I'm not casting aspersions on the building, not for a second, but my first time back there in twelve years and here again was the nagging pain, the tell-tale signs of fever, the extreme tiredness I'd had to work through at the Abbey before. Dammit!

No one asks you to work through illness or pain, but you do. In the 2005 production, I was so sick I was green. Impossible to hide that from a concerned cast and stage manager, who responsibly discussed cancelling the show. We didn't have understudies and they take health and safety very seriously. Not me, though. Not only am I an eejit, I'm also an eejit who acts and I knew the rules: *the show must go on.*

It's not just some vague sense of duty that makes you want to go on, regardless. Some of it is down to that, but that's only the tip of the theatrical iceberg. Some of it is that – even with a one-person show, with no other cast to consider – these things are team efforts and you're damned if you're letting the director, stage manager, publicity people, ticket-takers and ushers down. Even if they could use a night off. No! Most significant of all is the fact that you love what you do and you feel so lucky to be working that you just don't want to miss it, or diss it, by not showing up. So you show up. You bloody well show up. And the show somehow goes on.

If actors 100 per cent physically can't show up, others fill in, scripts in hand. I've seen shows continue after bomb scares or fire alerts. During power cuts. A show's what we're here to do, so a show's what's going to happen.

There's also Dr Theatre. Dr Theatre is the weird phenomenon that means that, even if your leg is falling off, a mad burst of adrenaline and some sort of wizardry cause the limb to reattach just long enough for you to perform. Voices lost temporarily return; sprained ankles are (unwisely) walked on, unfelt; fevers abate and mucus evaporates. The only charge for the doctor's visit is the crash that follows; the pain afterwards is hellish. But Dr Theatre gets you through your gig.

In 2005 the stage manager reluctantly gave in to my insistence and let me do the show. But, in truth, that night I was possibly too ill to make that call. It's a blur. The fabulous Aaron Monaghan was in the cast and he is so talented that he not only knew his own blocking, but mine too: hallucinating, I'd feel my elbow being grabbed and gently guided to whatever was the spot I was meant to be in. Thank heavens for Aaron, or I might have gone over the edge. Literally. Pain had me hovering about an inch above the boards and tilting towards the auditorium.

So when, last Monday, I felt a similar stab of pain, I didn't mess about. Straight to the (real) doctor. Got me some meds and a follow-up appointment.

But was I going to get through a run at our National Theatre pain-free? Apparently not. On Wednesday, the night before the first show, I woke in agony. No toughing this out. Paracetamol and screaming were doing nothing to ease it, so off with myself and the fella to A&E.

The hospital staff were brilliant and it wasn't too busy, which was great news because I was fairly sure that my agony wasn't long-term serious, so I'd be bumped if graver injuries came in. The pain was by now so severe I was no longer able to sit, stand or lie down, which didn't leave me a lot of options. There was talk of CT scans, of surgery, of '… if that's the case we'll whip you straight up to theatre …' 'NO!' I hissed through clenched teeth. 'Please, I can't go to theatre. I'm supposed to be on in THE theatre.' They looked at me with the kind of pity reserved for those detached from reality and I don't blame them. I swore to them that if I needed surgery, I'd come back Sunday. (Like that's how it works.) Those looks again. Those kind, 'This one's lost it' looks.

Anyway, good news! Massive doses of pain meds and the correct antibiotic later and I was fine. Well, maybe not fine, but fine enough to get my tush onto that stage. Which I did, at 8 p.m., on one hour's sleep.

They say that art is pain, that you have to bleed for it. Well, I've given it a good old go. But next time, I'd love not to have to put that to the physical test, if that's okay with you, Dr Theatre.

66

AM I USELESS?

I am forgettable. I am! This can be useful when the Biz is slow and I need to take on the odd spying gig, in a *Star Wars* 'These are not the droids you are looking for' way. Not so useful when it comes to getting back into a club/gig/play and they ask me to pay a second time. Not when practically everyone I've ever met calls me 'Tanya', or 'Tina', or 'Hey, You' on the second meet; they're all perfectly fine names ('Hey, You' especially), but the thing is, they're not mine.

I remember tackling it head-on at a comedy festival once. 'No, we haven't met,' said the tall, frosty woman I'd definitely met before. There must have been a spate of this happening at the time, because I'd had enough. I stood my ground. 'We have met,' I said. 'Remember? It was at the hot dog stand? Steve and Mike were there? There was that crash – the piano falling off the roof? You held onto my lapels and cried?' Instead of lying outright to save my ego or being in any way sound at all, she said, 'No. No, I still don't know you. Maybe it was dark?' 'It wasn't,' I said, standing on tiptoe to reach halfway to her elbow, where I hoped I might find my pride. 'Well, it's dark now,' she said, turning and sashaying off to what can only have been the ice palace from *Frozen*.

But that yucky moment was ages ago! These are happier times! It's Awards Season! The time when people get all dressed up to accept prizes, with impeccably whitened smiles and impossibly glowing skin despite being 'very tired'. They have to pretend they're delighted, even if they don't win the prize. But they're nominated. They're remembered. And it's such an honour. It's probably the burden of the honour that has them feeling so tired.

Being repeatedly told you're awesome must be brilliant. But now we've all evolved a crunchy shell of healthy, self-protecting cynicism, it must be weird too. Adulation must make for inner turmoil: it's not possible to be universally awesome, so maybe only some of those applauding you are ... right? Or maybe they're all wrong? Or maybe ... maybe they're lying?

Luckily, I don't have to worry about that existential dilemma. I've only won one thing, ever. Two things, if you count the painting competition when I was six – but everyone won something in that. Don't for one second think I'm consumed with bitterness, I'M NOT. Losing is my path. I accepted it ages ago.

Am I therefore 'a loser'? I hope not. But nor can I be said to be one of life's winners. (To clarify, we're talking competitions or competitive fields here. Or something like the lottery. I'm well aware how hard I've been hit with the privilege stick. I am a winner there.)

It was the late 1980s. (Yeah, here comes a story. Stick with Grandma.) As you'll have seen from the account of my fraught relationship with tennis in Chapter 12, I had an early morning summer job as a chambermaid at a Kinsale hotel. I used to cycle the four miles into town, serve Americans their breakfasts, clean rooms, then hang around until the tennis courts opened and play there all day before cycling home again. As you also may have read, I'm not ashamed to say that I got very, very good at tennis (and at cleaning toilets, but that's a story for another day). When the courts ran a tournament, I signed up. Surely, here was something I could win? Tournament week, I climbed steadily up the ladder, laying waste to people older than me, people taller than me (most people). I was in scorching form. And guess what? I only bloody won! I WON. I. Me. I WON. But, due to a technicality (someone else not turning up for a different match), it was decided that I was to play my defeated opponent again, straight away. On the back of much fry-serving, bed-making and pedalling, this time I flagged, and lost the re-match tie-break by two measly points. I was gutted.

If I'd originally been allowed just to come second – to lose – like normal, I'd have been fine. But the taste of the win, and the losing of it, broke me. I decided to never let losing break me again.

Of course winning isn't everything, but when so much is made of it in the showbiz world – BAM! FIZZ! WALLOP! WHO ARE YOU WEARING? – what if you never win? Your day to day, non-glitzy contribution can feel unimportant by comparison. Good, but not good enough. Even though the politics and PR involved in these things are well known, it can get under your skin.

I've never made it onto a shortlist; even if there were a 'Best at being Tara Flynn from Kinsale' award and I were on the judging panel, I'm pretty sure I wouldn't make the cut. And that's okay; the work is everything, must be everything. Prizes are sugary icing, the work is delicious cake. I still occasionally find myself wondering, though, if this means I'm really at the races? Could I be in the wrong stall, maybe? Is my jockey packing a few extra pounds? Am I even a horse?

Just know this: if I ever do win an award, tune in. I will keel over in shock, right there at the podium. That'll make for some pretty awesome television, or my name isn't Tanya Flynn.

67

CHEAP-ASS PRODUCERS

In films, showbiz agents are brilliant characters. You'd love to play one, like. A little bit seedy, they call everyone 'Darling!' in clipped voices down Bakelite phones from behind giant desks in improbable offices. They live for 'the deal' and would do anything for their client. Often, they have a cigar. Think Estelle, Joey's chain-smoking, bird's-nest-haired agent in *Friends*; Jane Plough in *Toast of London*; the never-seen Raymond Duck in *Withnail & I* – whose office Uncle Monty describes as 'Four floors up on the Charing Cross Road and never a job at the top of them.'

There rarely is. That's the reality of acting. Late at night, in dive bars the world over, actors slur the dire stats at each other: 'Just 10% of actors are working (as actors) at any one time. Or something.' Some get lucky and get a big job with nice money, but even then they don't know when the next audition will be, so that money has to last.

'Show' is the business with which I'm most familiar. But it seems there's a new phenomenon reaching far beyond the performing arts: we're all being asked to work for nothing.

It's a strange time in The Biz. It's all gone a little bit Black Market, a bit underground, a bit shit. People approach performers directly, even though they're not supposed to do that. You have an agent. They know this. And how do I know they know? Because you spend time and money making sure it's everywhere: on your CV, your website, and in every anecdote. 'Ask my agent', 'I'll have to run it past my agent', 'Get your people to talk to my people.'

And why won't prospective employers go through the professional channels? Money, of course. Agents will only ask for it for you. Some of it is undoubtedly for them (those cigars and desks don't pay for themselves), but the rest is what you'll need to pay your bills. It's almost as if they're suggesting the employer value your contribution – you know, the reason they called you in the first place?

Agents are a buffer; like most humans who want to work, performers are useless. We love what we do, so we get penalised for it. We need to be seen to be working, or we start to vanish from the marketplace like the McFly family photo in *Back to the Future*. Some producers have an unscrupulous belief we'll do it for a commodity known as 'exposure'. It's sometimes valuable, but until the banks develop exposure lodgement ATMs, it won't buy you many beans or electricity or soap.

It wasn't always thus, although I know this may be hard to believe for those newly arrived in the industry. People used to call your agent, you'd audition and, if you got the job, there'd be a contract with money written on it. Nowadays, such an occurrence is increasingly rare. And the effect is rippling outwards. There have never been so many free-admission gigs, the subconscious message to audiences being that what's being performed isn't of value. In telly terms, there's a worrying emphasis on cheap-to-make, sometimes mean-spirited hidden camera stuff, instead of paying writers and performers properly.

If you don't have the money to make a thing, don't make it. If you do, please talk to our agents.

I leave you with a script:

The Biz

We open on a dark alley. An actor, having finished their shift at literally any other job they could get, turns into it. Woman in trench coat follows him.

Woman: Hey kid.

The actor stops. Turns.

Actor: Who's there?

Stepping into the greenish light, inclining her hat brim so her face is visible, we realise the trench-coat woman is the Producer from earlier.

Producer/Woman: It's me.

Actor: You!

Producer: Yeah. Listen, kid. I got a job for you. A good one. Everyone will see it. You'll be the talk of the town.

Actor: You do?? Gee, that's swell, lady. I really need a job. I mean, really. Thank you. Here …

He hands her a card.

Actor: … my agent. Oh gee, I'm so excited.

She lets the card fall to the floor. Her gaze follows it.

Producer: Agent???

Actor (*proudly*): Yes ma'am.

Producer: You want me to talk to an *agent*? Come on, kid, get real. They'll only ask for money for you.

Actor: Well, yeah. Sure. It's a *job*, you said. I even get paid for my shitty one. I'm hungry to do what I do, but … I'm also just hungry.

His stomach growls. The Producer laughs. She picks up the card from the damp alley floor and rips it into tiny pieces. It's small, and now damp, so this takes considerable skill. She manages it.

Producer: Don't worry. We'll get someone else to do it. Someone not so … precious.

She ticky-tacks away in expensive stilettos. The Actor spreads his arms, turns his face upwards into the rain and the camera cranes up and away, like in every movie since The Shawshank Redemption.

Fin.

68

WHAT IS THE ARTS, JOXER?

Yet again in Ireland, someone has been forced to start a petition. With the government not seeming to care, more and more people are taking things into their own hands. Who knows if petitions even work? Does anyone read them? Do they actually stop people taking any further, possibly more direct, action? Whether they're ultimately effective or not, they've become a part of daily life when it seems the lads in the shit-shiny suits and gaping shirts don't give a damn about a damn thing.

They don't. That's become clear. Don't give me any crap after yet another general election about giving them time to prove themselves, *shur, aren't they only in the door?* NO! It's the same old faces, again. The parties in power don't even pretend to be different from each other, so it's almost impossible to know who to vote for. Will some radical new alternative get in if we vote for them? Will they change once they are in, or try to work the status quo from the inside? It's still the status quo – is there any difference? So we're left with the same lads in the same suits, feeling untouchable. It's almost like having a monarchy. And at least if we had a king our parades might have more horses in them. Everyone likes horses. Although the politics are almost as crappy as what they leave behind them.

Being shocked by the attitude of any 'new' government made up of the same old parties to the major issues (mental health, human rights, housing) makes me a fool, because they're nothing if not consistent. But how can they be so disconnected? Have the cozy surroundings of Leinster House been soundproofed? Can they not hear us? It's obvious they have no idea what the country is screaming for. The world, rapping our knuckles again and again. Are they so full of carvery beef (Irish, of course, because 'the economy!') that indigestion slows them, keeping them out of step with pretty much everything?

Feeling powerless and unheard, people set up petitions. If nothing else, the solidarity of seeing your name among others is a good first step.

Some issues are more pressing than others. But, in 2016, theatre practitioner John O'Brien became the private citizen mobilising us to beg our government not to sideline the Arts. In a country that pimps our culture unmercifully to lure tourism and business (*economy! economy! economy!*) there's something really seedy about the removal of this standalone government department. Every time there's an overseas visitor, dancers, singers and poets are wheeled out. We shuffle tourists and dignitaries around our galleries, point out the vibrant street art, remind them that we're the funniest storytellers of them all. 'Our Lenny! Our John! Our Colm! Our Emma! Our Saoirse!' we bleated during Oscar week, through mouthfuls of popcorn and pride. Fishamble have represented us at the Olivier awards; half the West End at any given moment has an Irish background. And sure aren't we the queens of literature altogether?

As Lenny Abrahamson tweeted when the department was sidelined: 'Despite all the lip service, it's clear from lack of action that the Irish political class neither understands nor values the arts.'

No taoiseach can leave the country without a fleet of Irish dancers and at least one *sean nós* genius in his entourage. No one else is allowed to leave without a tin whistle in their pocket. There's a harp on our passports – on all our official documents. When you pay tax, the little symbol seems to say that even though things may be shite, our rich heritage is valued and celebrated.

Nah. Not so much. They don't rate it.

Then again, we've seen other ruthless cuts that show they don't really care about our bodies or minds. Why would they give a shit about our souls?

This isn't about a shakedown for grants (although some theatres, festivals, etc., won't survive without them). It's about support for the very expression of who we are. Depressing that, on top of their own inaction, the suit lads don't rate the only spaces where many of the issues they wish to ignore are being voiced right now. But of course they don't. Deep, important needs are being expressed artistically in a way we haven't seen here in decades. Here, perhaps more than anywhere, the Arts have been where the seeds of social change have taken root. Maybe that's the problem. Maybe they're scared. It won't stop them going to the next gallery opening or quoting Irish writers in their speeches, but artists seem to scare them. In terms of entertainment, they seem to want nothing more than to be in the Dáil bar, talking about themselves, flashing their whitened-for-the-election-poster teeth. No wonder they don't rate us.

Well, that's okay, lads. The artsy magicians out here in the real world are making some noise. They're not here to entertain. They make magic. Look out.

69

THE SECRET OF SUCCESS

'When did you know you'd made it?' the interviewer asked, innocently, his Zoom recorder whirring away between us. (Forever and always, I will imagine recording devices to *whirr*, because that's what tape recorders used to do. It's not nostalgia; it's some sort of weird conditioning. Like the way they added scratchy vinyl sounds to digital tracks before vinyl came back: if you'd heard it often enough, there would always be something missing without it. My brain adds it back in.)

But I digress. We were talking about making it. Every now and again, I'll get asked about it, like this young man just had and although my impulse is to laugh, I end up sounding tetchy. I'm not tetchy about it, not at all. It's quite a flattering question, really. It means the asker perceives me to have achieved something. Which is nice. If there is tetchiness, even a little, it comes from knowing what I know about my life, and not wanting to sound ungrateful or dismissive of their success-perception, while still answering accurately. Back to the interview.

When I got my first book onto the actual shelves of actual shops, I nearly cried. Oh, I am lying to you, young man: there was no 'nearly' about it. I cried buckets, regularly. It was too much. A dream come true. I thought I might burst. Friends were happy for me, family relieved I had something more to show for *all this* than a few curling posters and yellowing theatre programmes in the attic.

Then the most surprising thing happened. I started to get messages from people I didn't know. It's one of the strangest things about becoming a face people recognise. It's often one of the nicest things too: people you don't know having opinions and pre-conceptions about you can be weird, but their taking the time to get in touch is a privilege. Sometimes the preconception is that you're so big for your boots and fancy that you won't personally see their message, let alone be blown away and grateful for it. Sometimes the preconception is that you're an alien 'celeb type' and know everybody who's ever been on the pages of *RSVP*, when that isn't actually a place. (Actually, because of the size of Ireland, you do know many of them, but where you know them from is the shops. Or you went to school with their cousin, or something.) Unless you work hard at that aspect, life doesn't become a celebrity whirl the second you do a bit of work that brings you to people's attention.

More weirdness: money. People ask you for it. This isn't limited to charities asking you to show up and donate your time, maybe do a free show; that's fine. Great, in fact. That's a lovely thing, good use of a platform. I'm talking about people I've never met, young man, just asking for money. *Gimme it*, like. And not just *FundMy-Ass*-type requests (though it's embarrassing enough to have to turn them down because you just donated to your pal who's been trying to make an album for ten years and that's your funding capability maxed out). Strangers came out of nowhere to ask me to invest in their business ventures, in a week in which I'd probably been planning to invest in not having the electricity cut off. I end up having to explain – to strangers – that I can't afford it right now. Bit of a reddener to have to say it out loud. And then they don't believe you. Especially if they've just seen you looking glossy on TV. Here's a behind-the-curtain bit of goss: while promoting your own product (which is a massive part of the game), you aren't paid for those appearances. Someone might have fixed your hair before you went on, giving the illusion of not having been dragged backwards though a hedge, but you're only there to beg people to buy the thing you have out there, so you might have money someday. So it's nice that people assume you're successful like they think you are. But it pops your fragile bubble when you realise they're disappointed: you aren't successful in the way they thought, and you start to wonder whether you should be.

So I'm glad you asked that question, young man. To me, having *made it* means ease, being able to draw a breath without it catching from stress. Success is having guarantees that, a year from now, you'll still be working, still able to pay the mortgage. It's not recognition – awards can be flavour of the month or driven by publicity machines. They don't always lead to real, liveable success – especially if you're one of life's second-placers. *Making it* isn't recognition in terms of people having heard of you: I mean, maybe they've heard of you, but hate you. And just because you've heard of someone doesn't mean everyone has; this can lead to cringey half-intros down the pub. I prefer to assume that no one's heard of me: then we're all starting from a healthy place.

I might feel like I've made it if someday I manage to have a healthy savings account for rainy days. It might not be going-into-business-ventures-with-cheeky-random-strangers healthy, but healthy enough to see a little bit ahead, make some plans. I might feel like I've made it when I get seen for jobs, not hear about them when they're already in the can. I might feel like I've made it when I'm not still being asked – like everyone in the business, maybe everyone everywhere – to work for little or nothing, *because you love it*. I might feel like I've made it when I've figured out what my next project is and how to make it happen. Till then, making it is, for me, STILL BEING HERE. Still in the business you started out in? You're making it.

Holding down another job to make staying in that business possible? You're making it.

If you hardly have time to write or make or play your instrument because of other commitments to pay the bills, but you find that time somehow and just do it, that's making it.

Shout out to everyone who gets up at 5 a.m. to do their creative thing before working a whole day, getting kids to school. Or squeezing out a few lines after midnight.

If you're managing, at all, you're making it. So few of us are managing. If you are, that's like a star on the Walk of Fame. Count your lucky star.

And, somehow, young man, I am still here. But believe me, I'm not off next to a nail salon to have real diamond chips stuck onto my talons.

Zoom recorder whirrs.

When will I feel I'm an adult? When will I know what I'm doing, confidently putting one grown-up foot in front of another? When do we stop being scared?

I'll let you know, young man, as soon as it happens. Because it's not when you get your first job. Not when you buy a flat, or learn to drive. It's not when you lose a parent. It's not even when you find yourself staring down a half century, wondering how the time flew by so fast. It was only yesterday we were still pressing *record* and *play*.

It's best never to assume anyone is sorted. We are all all kinds of fucked up. Dreams are great, but there's more than one way for them to come true. 'All or nothing' is overrated. 'Something' is nothing to be ashamed of.

Did you get all that, young man? Lovely. It was nice to meet you. Of course I'll pay for the tea.

FAITH(LESS)

A CHAT AND A CUPPA WITH ST PATRICK

This last section is all about faith. You 'gotta have' it, as George Michael says, and for centuries what Ireland had was the Catholic religion – and not just when it came to church. Our hospitals, education, even our laws are intertwined with it. But the country has gradually become more and more secular in recent years, so where does that leave us, with all our Catholic teaching? (To this day most schools in Ireland have what they call a 'Catholic ethos'.) Where does it leave me? I thought it'd be enlightening to catch up with someone with his finger on the pulse. Our patron saint: St Pat himself.

As he's been reclusive of late, it takes me a while to track him down and, when I do, he asks me not to disclose his location. So I won't. But let's just say it was pretty Meath-sy to find. The property is gated, and the voice that answers and buzzes me in is surprisingly spry. He tells me to park behind the property. I do.

It takes some time to walk around to the front of the house. I say 'house', though it's more of an earthen mound with a round tower sticking up out of it, impressive in its own way. Much like the man himself.

He answers the door wearing pyjamas and slippers and that famous sweet smile. 'Sorry,' he says, 'I'm just up. It's been quite the week and I'm not as young as I used to be! Takes me a while to get down the tower steps.'

I have to give him this. It's barely a week since the St Patrick's

Festival, focused on 17 March, his Day and busiest time. As I step into the tower, I realise with some surprise that, despite his being such a familiar figure, I've never heard his voice before. It's hard to place his accent. Not Irish, not … well, it's not Irish, but there's definitely a hint of the ancient about it. He gathers up newspapers strewn here and there, all bearing front page pictures of Paddy's Day parades from around the world, and gestures for me to sit. I remark that I'm surprised to see that nothing – not the leather couch, not the stripy pyjamas, not even the potted plant – is green. For a second, the twinkle leaves his eye. I've made some kind of *faux pas* but it appears he's too polite to tell me what it is. He is, after all, a saint.

Or is he? Once he has served me tea (he doesn't drink, he says, and won't keep alcohol in the house) and settled into the large throne that forms the centrepiece of the room, rather than tiptoe around the most controversial question, I decide to open with it.

Tara Flynn: Isn't it true that you're no longer a saint, or that you never were one in the first place, or something?

Saint Patrick: (*chuckles*) Straight in! You don't mess about, do you?

TF: I think it's something people are curious about.

SP: I don't pay much attention to titles. After all, some of the most atrocious people in history have been sainted, or are about to be. There are some clubs it's better not to be a member of. The celebrity has been fun, so long as I have this place to get away from it all. I get a lot of heat one week of the year. For the rest of it, they leave me more or less alone.

TF: So you're not a saint, really?

SP: There you go, with your titles again! Let's leave it at this: how many people do you know with thrones in their living room?

I admit I don't know any, and agree not to push it.

TF: The whole snakes thing ...?

SP: Oh God! The snakes! That was a schoolboy prank that got legs – unlike them! Sure, there were never any snakes in Ireland. About nine hundred years ago I was in charge of bringing a basket of eels to a friend's stag do (a weekend hunting actual stags). We were going to drop them down the groom's tunic. En route, I fell asleep near a river and they slithered away. The lads were devastated that the prank was off, and I got an unmerciful slagging, which stuck. But most crushing of all was my own disappointment in myself. Since then, no more mead for me. I get a lot more done during the day. And I haven't lost an eel – not to mention a snake – since.

TF: What's your day like?

SP: I'm up very early. Not this week, of course, I get a lie-in shortly after the Big Day, but usually I am. In the week of My Festival, I have a lot of public appearances to make. Like St Nicholas, I have to employ the odd lookalike, but I try to personally make as many as I can. The rest of the year is mainly spent in preparation. Sit-ups, that kind of thing.

TF: Tell us something we wouldn't know about you.

SP: I invented the shamrock. Actually invented it. I wanted to teach the whole Holy Trinity thing, *yada yada*, and I picked up a four-leaf clover, secretly pulling off one of the leaves to make my point. Ireland's natural clover used to be the four-leaf clover; so, to give the story credence, I have to go around and pull the one leaf off all of them. Ta-da! Shamrock! Something local to take in a bowl when visiting foreign dignitaries. Pulling those single leaves off is a year-round job. Detractors say that's why Ireland has had no luck of late, but that's just silly superstition.

My elderly host is visibly starting to flag, but before I finish my tea and take my leave, I have to ask.

TF: Women, St Pat. Do they figure in your story at all?

He tents his fingers and muses before answering.

SP: I have Twitter, you know. I read what people say: that if I hadn't come along, women in Ireland might be in a lot better position than they have been. I don't know if that's true – there were always those who saw them as chattel – but I can tell you what I think. Irish women have had to put up with an awful lot of dung, so fair play to ye for sticking around at all. Also, St Bridget is a very good friend of mine.

TF: St Bridget is still alive?

SP: Oh, she's at every feminist rally. In disguise, of course – she can't give the game away. But look down next time ... she'll be the one wearing home-made rush sandals.

He yawns. It really is time to go. As he shows me to the mound door, one last question. 'Why the no green?'

'It's not my colour,' he says, 'I'm more of an autumn.'

I know there must be more to this glorious mystery, but he slowly shuts the door, holding my gaze as he does so. There's something about Patrick, but all I know for certain is this: it's not what you think it is.

71

NO-GHOST STORY

I don't believe in ghosts. Here's why.

My Dad died a few years ago and he is gone.

I know where he is: he's in County Clare, in the village where he was born, his ashes now on his mother's grave, exactly as he wished. We went there with the extended family on a sunny April day and there were poems and music, a second funeral, a second celebration of his life. Drinks after. Plenty of slagging. So, I know where he is. And whenever I can, I go back. Back to Clare to walk along the graveyard wall like he taught me when we'd go to visit his mother, when I went there with him, a shortcut to her spot that meant you didn't have to risk walking on anyone else's grave if you were at all unsteady or unsure. I know precisely where the grave is. Know the view down the hill, the little dip towards the village, another hill beyond. All green and peaceful. It's a lovely view.

I know that not to believe in ghosts is a deeply unpatriotic thing for an Irish woman to admit. Half our tourist industry is built on haunted houses or turrets from which people have hurled themselves on their wedding nights, meaning their spirits appear there still. The White Lady did just that, off Charles Fort in Kinsale. She's meant to hang around the ramparts of the fort, still looking for her new husband, who'd mistakenly been shot hundreds of years before. 'Bet you wouldn't stay in the fort overnight!' we used to dare each other as kids. You bet right, my friend. I wouldn't have stayed there for a hundred pounds. I was scared to tangle with the White Lady; but I'd probably have died anyway – of anticipation and fright.

There's a hotel named after her. It has a disco attached which was the scene of much snogging and drink taking. *Black Russians.* What were we thinking? Especially as my father would usually be there to pick us up and drive us the country road home. We would have preferred to stay in town 'with friends'. He saw right through that one. The disco ended at 1 a.m. and if we didn't hit the car by 1.03 a.m. there was WAR. No discos for us for ages. A fate worse than death.

Punctuality is something he left me. Dad always used to say, 'Leave time for two punctures. What if the spare tyre is flat? Leave time for two punctures, then you'll make your flight.' I didn't drive at the time and had been on a plane maybe once, but I saw what he was saying. Now, the worst possible punishment I can mete out to myself is to be late. Believe me, if I'm late for you and it makes you cross, your wrath has nothing to the beating up I'm giving to myself as I sit in traffic or hop foot to foot on a crowded bus. I need to be there five minutes early. Five minutes early = on time. Five minutes late = opprobrium, silent night driving and no discos. Nobody wants that.

My dad was difficult, uncompromising and our relationship was often strained. But that doesn't change the earth-shattering nature of the space left by a presence like his when it goes. He was a giant, and not always a friendly one. He was often forbidding even to those who weren't related to him. He was very tall (I got his nose, but none of his stretch), stubborn (I did get that), funny (I am that too, sometimes). He absolutely did not care what people thought. Sometimes people thought awful things and I found myself siding with them – the people, not my dad. But he didn't give a single solitary fuck. He would often phrase it in those words too, in his deep, clear voice, hammering every syllable for emphasis. A voice that could charm you or chill you, depending on his mood.

The sky comes off. That's what happens when a parent dies. Like a roof in a storm, your whole sky peels back and leaves you tiny and exposed. Surprised too, even though you know that's foolish. Even when it's been a long-expected thing. When my dad died, I couldn't tell the time. I looked from my watch to a wall-clock for confirmation, but neither made sense. My ears rang. My knees went. I couldn't tell the time.

He was gone. Dementia had already taken him part of the way, but now he was really gone. *Gone* gone. The glint in the eye. The fierceness. The intelligence. The fun. All gone.

I used to be superstitious, now I'm not. I used to wonder if doors slamming or bumps in the night were souls of the departed having wicked fun at my expense. Now I suspect nothing but the wind.

Because late at night now, when I ask my dad a question, he's not there. And if he were, I promise, I would know. He'd make it known. That presence cannot go unless it's gone. I don't believe in ghosts any more. I wish I did.

72

IT'S LENT? PASS THE CHOCOLATE

It's Lent, is it? I always forget. It used to be such a fun, guilt-ridden time but now it's more likely to be used as some kind of heavenly detox. *Try the new forty-day fast! Just swap dessert for desert and watch a whole new you emerge!*

The idea is that you could give something up, or you could do something positive for forty days (not giving a fuck, for instance), like Jesus did in the desert. If he'd cared about what people thought, he'd have jumped at that fancy sports car as soon as Satan offered it. (To be honest, the details have gotten a bit fuzzy since I realised I didn't believe in God, but these are still badass stories.)

It has to be said, there was a great sense of communal misery when we all used to 'do' Lent together. We took the thing that gave us the most pleasure – smoking, drinking, Jaffa cakes; *WAIT, WHY WAS SEX NEVER MENTIONED?* – and agreed to give it up. Everyone had their secret stashes, of course. No one believed anyone ever really went forty days without the good shit. You'd have a small guilt-pile somewhere, for whenever you couldn't cope. (If you think it's not possible to guilt-pile sex, you haven't done it right.)

Hard to believe now, but this was bonding, watercooler stuff (you were allowed not to give up hydration). 'What have you given up for Lent?' was an ice-breaker with strangers in shops or on trains. It probably went some way to preventing violent crimes – 'I can't rob him now – he's suffering too!' Let's ignore for the moment the fact that if you hadn't given anything up and were bold enough to say so, there would be repercussions. Very, very judgey ones.

These are different times and most people have given up giving up. Although this means forty days of fun, like normal, we've lost that community of misery, that bond of lack. Does that make Lent itself a bit, y'know, *tempting*? Obviously, it's not possible to conjure up faith you've lost, or never had, but there are definitely times I miss that free pass into the Virtue Club. That chocolate-starved nod of recognition at the bus-stop. Now, chocolate sales continue after Ash Wednesday – boom, even – and people have even been known to buy Easter Eggs before Holy Week. Just a few short years ago, this would have made *The Six One News*.

'What happens if you break Lent?' asked an Aussie friend once. 'The Easter Bunny doesn't come?'

'No!' I screamed, high on no-chocolate. 'Much worse than that. This is no softly softly Santa-style approach.'

He munched his Crunchie, oblivious. It was too late for him. So while he and others mocked us from their treat-filled mouths, they didn't understand the power of abstaining together. The clear complexions and consciences. Jam jars slowly filling with coins that might have gone on beer. That all sounds alluring, doesn't it? It'd take quite a dose of guilt to turn you off it.

Although I'm vegetarian now, as a child I ate what I was given and was grateful for it as the law commands. That meant sand-wiches and school milk for lunch. What went into the sandwich was leftovers, or jam. Nice jam, but there was no waste in our house (you'd use the jar for coins later) and no fancy shop-shit either. I don't think I had a fish finger till I was eleven; you wouldn't get any leftovers out of them. Sliced ham? That was for town funerals, when people were too consumed with grief to honey-glaze one themselves, not for a weekday lunch.

One such weekday, I brought a bacon sandwich to school. It certainly wasn't meant as a statement. It was a Wednesday, I'll never forget it. But what we'd all forgotten at home was that it was Ash Wednesday (the wasteful single-pancake use of eggs the night before should have been a giveaway). In case, like us, you've forgotten, Ash Wednesday is a fast day. Not that it passes quickly: you're not supposed to eat. Well, they changed the rules so you can eat now, but only dry toast. Well, they changed it again so it's not just dry toast any more, but you must eat simply. No meat. Most of all, *NO MEAT*. We didn't know. Or we knew but we'd forgotten. And then somebody in my class sang like a holy canary. A canary you'd have to call Judas. Judas the Canary.

I was dragged up in front of the class. This was far worse than when you'd miss the odd Mass and not know the sermon when asked for a recap by the nuns. On this particular Wednesday, we got a lecture with me as the subject, all about respect and holy days. I returned, humiliated and sandwichless, to my desk. No lunch for me, aged eight, *because Jesus*.

Even as the tears sailed down my face (providing a little salt for sustenance), I had a feeling this wasn't what He'd had in mind when He'd turned down the fancy car. This was not my club. Tempting as it is to belong, I realised that Lent just wasn't going to be my thing. So please, pass the chocolate.

73

IDEOLOGY AND DICK MOVES ON HOLY WEEK

To be honest, I'd been writing about something else; about eggs and pagans and Easter and whatever is your spring festival of choice, but news of yet another terror attack changed that. I started thinking about thinking itself, really, and how we – with all our different backgrounds and beliefs – do it.

These grim terrorist events took place in what Christians (and lots of the rest of us, out of habit) know as Holy Week, but let's afford no intended symbolism to the terrorists. We don't care what they intended. We give them no oxygen.

This grimness is not new. Attacks like these happen all around the world all the time. Closer to home, I remember when the IRA was so active you'd get searched going into the airport – even if you weren't travelling, even if you were five. Even in Cork, where thankfully little ever blew up apart from word of famous visiting jazz musicians, come October.

Are such events more numerous than before? Hard to say. A hundred years ago they didn't have the firepower, it's true, but by the same token you could vanish in your own village and never be found. If something didn't happen in your village, you might never hear about it – especially if you weren't much of a reader. Today, insta-reporting brings every detail, fact and figure of the unfolding anguish to our fingertips, and we scroll eagerly for more.

The villains of the awful piece change, but the piece goes on, decade after decade, like one of those blockbuster West End plays – *The Mousetrap*, or one of those eternal touring versions of *Les Mis* – where even the actors are tired of it and the costumes were originally made for someone else.

Pointing fingers at a particular faith or ethnicity is, therefore, pointless. Creating an 'other' is the terrorists' goal, and why play into their goal-mouth? (I'm not exactly sure what a goal-mouth is; hopefully not some kind of sexual euphemism that's going to put you off your chocolate eggs.)

I've seen many pieces highlighting the common thread in so many violent attacks committed down through the years: religion. But I think it's too easy to blame religion, when clearly most people of faith live quiet lives with no desire to control anyone else. But boy, oh boy, is extreme ideology a dick. The more blindly someone clings to one – be it Catholicism or raw juicing or grammar fascism – the less compassion and reason they seem to have. Idealistic ideologists seem capable of tuning out others' suffering, not to mention being oblivious to quite how insignificant the odd misplaced apostrophe really is. Following dogma removes the need to question, and questioning is what helps you to remember that you and what you believe might not be … well, might not be all that.

I used to love Holy Week ritual: Stations of the Cross, special ceremonies, endless rounds of confession. I tried so hard to be a good girl. I did try. The game was rigged, though: I would never be good enough, not having been born the Virgin Mary herself. I could confess several thousand times a day, but it still wouldn't count. Sure look, hadn't I already ruined Lent that time by almost eating bacon on Ash Wednesday? (see Chapter 72). And wasn't I a woman? I was never going to be able to pray hard enough to be as good as they dictated. Even though they certainly couldn't have been said to be behaving according to their own impossible standards.

Eventually, my questioning led me away from it all. But I still miss the incense and incantations, and I envy people who find comfort in their faith.

When I moved to Britain, years ago, I remember asking if the gym would be open on Good Friday. 'Of course!' came the bewildered reply. Not only was the gym not shut, but I'm sure they put up some kind of motivational posters to reflect the day: 'Every Friday's a Good Friday to work out!' 'Don't forget to Cross train!'

I don't know if they did. I didn't end up going. I went to the pub instead, because (unlike in Ireland) it was open and I could.

I don't mean any disrespect, and in the greater scheme of things, Ireland's Good Friday licensing laws (which are soon set to be a thing of the past) are about as significant as the odd misplaced apostrophe. But in Britain, as many people as went to the pub on Good Friday will be in church on Easter Sunday, singing their excellent hymns; they just don't expect you to do it too. Which is just as well – that's a heck of a lot of hymns to learn in a weekend. It's almost as if it's accepted that whether they go to the pub on the Friday or not – or whether you do – doesn't affect their faith. Hmmm.

One size of thinking does not fit all. So, here's my wish for Ireland, for the world: let's acknowledge that imposing ideology on anyone else is a dick move. The symbolic gesture of limiting or banning anything based on just one set of beliefs reaches much further than the snug. It can put people at risk. Let's move forward together instead.

Whether that's to the church or to the pub is your business.

74

THE MARCH OF THE CATHOLICS

I womanned the HeadStuff Twitter account once and the feeling of pure power surging through me was incredible, I'm not going to lie. At my fingertips, the possibility of directing people to what might be of interest to them (i.e. me), nosying around older articles I'd missed but sharing only the humour ones, capable of bringing down the organisation's entire reputation with a few ill-considered blasts. I didn't, though. I'm not evil – although I spent a good deal of time revealing the true nature of the HeadStuff bosses. (Evil. They keep us contributors in a cupboard, telling us to type faster.)

As those who were following that weekend know, I was in Kinsale while I was curating the account. It's where I grew up and where my mum still lives. I shared a few off-the-beaten-track photos the postcards would never show you. I'm very proud of my hometown. On a break from tweeting about HeadStuff podcasts people should check out, I went to a café near Mum's (this does not narrow it down; everything's near) for a coffee and a sit in the sunshine. All morning I'd been hearing bagpipes and wondering what the hell they were doing here? Was there some sort of Scottish Wild Geese festival I hadn't heard about? Was someone super fancy getting married? Or was it a bagpipe convention that had decided to take things outdoors to delight the rest of us as much as anyone who'd go to a bagpipe convention would think we'd be delighted by bagpipes? None of the above. As I sipped my delicious coffee and sunned my face, proudly eavesdropping on American tourists saying how beautiful the town was, they came.

Marching round the corner in their finery, pipers piping, they came: the Corpus Christi procession.

If you're not Catholic (even though in Ireland we all are, even those of us who aren't), I should explain that this is a celebration by the faithful of 'the Real Presence of Christ in the Eucharist'. It comes a specific amount of time after Easter which only a priest or a maths genius can properly explain – something about adding and subtracting full moons and other faiths' feast-days. Anyway, that specific amount of time had been the Thursday before, it seems, with the celebratory procession arranged for that Sunday. In Kinsale, the procession is always after 12 noon Mass, the coolest of all the Masses. All the recent first communicants wear their communion outfits again and everyone gets dressed up accordingly: you don't want to be outshone by a natty seven-year-old. The priest wears some really swishy robes and is walked around town under a kind of awning which is actually not for him, but for the Holy Eucharist – i.e. what the faithful believe to be the actual body of Christ Himself, in wafer form, in a star-shaped glass casing or 'monstrance'. I guess no one – not even Jesus – is immune to our strengthening UV rays, so the monstrance/awning arrangement is probably wise.

And today the UV rays were beating down. The pipers stopped piping and the familiar drone of call-and-response prayer took over. I guess it was the rosary, I can't be sure any more. It's a long time since I last prayed. I hadn't even remembered it was Corpus Christi – if the nuns heard that, I'd have been so in for it. See, I had the full whammy: full Catholic convent school education, all the sacraments possible – sad ones (ash); happy ones (kissing bishops' rings). I knew my Catechism back to front and some of the girls got off lessons the odd time to serve the priest tea in the convent parlour or to sing 'Ave Maria' at a nun's funeral. They desperately tried to recruit us when it came time to leave school. The boys were sent 'up the courts' to play some game or other and we got a separate talk from a cool nun in the audio-visual room about how great being a nun was and how we should do it. My whole family – my whole country, at the time – was Catholic.

I did my very best to believe, but I just couldn't manage it. These days, the term 'Anti-Catholic' is sometimes flung at me as an insult. Let me assure you, sir or madam: I am not anti-Catholic. I am a fucking full-blown Catholic. Confession, candles, incense, scapulars. Despite now being excommunicated – more on which in Chapter 75 – I know my shit.

As I got older and the Church scandal revelations accelerated and the loosening of its grip forced some seriously shady attempts to retain it, my lack of faith deepened. It was not without some envy, however, that I watched the procession curl past last Sunday, now smaller than when I was a kid, the pipers kicking in after what I can only assume from the tone of the drone was the end of a 'Sorrowful Mystery'. It must be comforting to have such ritual, such belief that the buck doesn't stop with you and that there's forgiveness and reward in the next life.

Or you can sit with the sun warming your face and be grateful for coffee, for love and the moment that you're in.

75

THE CLUB

Let's talk about how I became a Catholic in the first place. This is how it works: I was born and I wasn't a Catholic yet and then I was baptised in a rush and then I *was* a Catholic, supposedly until I die and absolutely ages after. Them's the club rules. This stuff is meant to last forever. Long after you've departed the mortal plane, you're meant to be reaping the benefits or living the consequences (*afterliving* them?) of how you spent your life and whether or not the Vatican would have approved of it. They've gotten rid of a few of the supernatural planes, so it's kind of hard to keep up, but rules are still rules. Limbo's gone, which is annoying, because who doesn't love to dance? But for simplicity's sake, best just to stick with the enduring concepts of heaven and hell. They're still eternally there. For now.

Anyway, I've been excommunicated. I enjoy saying it – it appeals to my sense of drama. I've been excommunicated. I can't go for communion. I can't be buried in a churchyard. I am going to hell.

The Pope didn't do it – the Pope's never heard of me, which is a shame. Nothing was nailed to giant oak doors, as far as I know. I don't think they even made any leaflets about it, to read aloud from church steps or even just tack to a parish noticeboard. It's not like Equity's blacklist, where they publish a clutch of dodgy, avoid-worthy, cheap-ass producer geezers in the back of every newsletter. No scrolls were unfurled before townspeople, no candles extinguished, no bells rung (or silenced) and no decrees were issued. But none of that changes the fact.

I was excommunicated automatically when I had an abortion. Them's the rules! Now, Pope Francis has recently said that penitent women can be welcomed back into the Church. But hussies like me, who are grateful for the care we received from non-judgemental medical professionals – we can never come back. It's this kind of absolutist stuff that breaks people. I count myself lucky that I had already fallen away from the Church and its teachings long before my excommunication.

But being kicked out of a club into which you'd been granted automatic membership still sucks. It was yours for the losing. Looking up other reasons for automatic excommunication, though, I realise that, in actuality, staying in the club is no mean feat. You can get kicked out for all kinds of stuff: from not belie-ving certain teachings, all the way up to physically attacking the Pope. Not everyone gets close enough to try that one, and there aren't many who'd want to hurt an aul' lad in a Plexiglass car any-way. So, although you can't help what you believe – and coercion hasn't ever really been effective as a way to get people to believe in things – it's still a case of 'out you go'. The touch of Church boot to our heathen arses is swift and sore.

Being kicked out now isn't as bad as in the olden days. There was no ceremony for my ejection; no one decried me from an altar (at least, not initially and not by name). News of my excommuni-cation elicits little more than a shrug and a laugh as opposed to the officially prescribed shunning. There's been very little actual shun-ning to be honest, although I wouldn't push my luck. I wouldn't wear my 'Heretics R Us' T-shirt to Midnight Mass, demanding wafer at the altar rails or anything.

I have no ill feelings towards the club. It's just far too exclusive for me. You might say I don't want to be a member of any club that wouldn't have me as a member. I'm aware that this re-working of a

Groucho quote doesn't quite work, but I mean it. Any club whose foundations are love and charity, but which essentially keeps saying 'except for you' is a club that might just have lost its way.

For all its well-documented transgressions, defenders of the faith (and the wealthy business that underpins it) will ask us to bear in mind all the good the Church has done. Hospitals. Schools. Right. Of course. But we never had an option here in Ireland to try any other kind of governance for these. So it's kind of a trick question, don't you think? Have there been good people in the clergy? Hell, yes! The nuns who taught me were legends. I mean, they were nuns, they had to teach us all the conservative, Vatican-y stuff, but most of them were kind, strong women. I've heard many of the younger ones have since left the order. This makes me sad (if not surprised), because I'm sure it was a traumatic and difficult realisation. A corporation (you heard me) famous for the historic abuses of women doesn't really get to keep great women any more. And yes, there are wonderful priests. There are brothers not hitting everyone a flake, we get it. The priest who said my dad's funeral Mass was gentle towards family members who admitted straight up that we weren't believers, so we wouldn't be participating, but we would be respectful observers. I couldn't tell him at the time that I was excommunicated. I didn't want to shock him; he was being so nice.

But I came very close to hurling it in the face of another priest, the man who gave my father the Last Rites. He was one of those older gentlemen who resents his weakened power: he would not leave me in respectful observation. I didn't object to his being there, in fact I stood back to give him room. He asked if I'd like to anoint my father. Deeply uncomfortable, already in the throes of grief, I said, 'No, thank you'.

'You will,' he said, like an even holier Mrs Doyle.

He grabbed my wrist, dipped my fingers in the oil and made me make the sign of the cross on my dying dad's head. I shook with shock and anger. Though trembling, I froze in disbelief, which was useful; it stopped me from speaking. All the while, I had a secret that could have stopped all this. Yet despite the fact that the man showed no respect for me or my beliefs, I chose not to give him a heart attack by telling him he'd made a Church outlaw a momentary minister. I doubt that'd go down so well over brandy in the parochial house.

Long before the scandals, long before my own plummet from grace, I simply didn't believe what the Church taught, the way they taught it. I had nothing to lose by having my membership revoked. The good stuff, the *Love Thy Neighbour* stuff? That's in most religions you come across; it's a good tenet even if you live religion-free. I just didn't believe I was better than my LGBT friends, or than people who needed visits from The Missions, or even than Protestants, which was weird, because they were usually the ones in town with the Bond-villain yachts. In case you're wondering, I'm not in the yacht club either. I might not be better than any club members, but I'll tell you what: I'm certainly no worse.

76

FAITH

It seems harder to do an end-of-year stock-take or reflection right now. As a calendar year draws to a close, I usually relish the excuse to focus on light at a time when it's getting dark at freelance-lunchtime, to think about the supposed real gifts of the season: peace, love, hope. Even faith. Finding evidence of any of these has been a challenge of late.

But still, the year's end comes. Only now we have to do it without Bowie. There do seem to have been some essential people holding the universe together and now we have to do it all without them. Without Carrie Fisher (about whom I think nearly every day, though she's not mentioned in these essays), without George Michael (who is). So we need to help each other to find those gifts. They're not readily under the tree any more. But they are out there. I'm sure of it.

Peace. I don't know if you remember a time (it wasn't long ago) when, even if people had differences of opinion, they gave each other space to live that difference? Now the goal seems to be to offend, to wound, to *win*. Globally, lives are reduced to collateral damage in debate or hypothetical argument. At the end of this year, I wish you peace. (Although, if you're spending time with family it's highly unlikely. My advice is to get the Christmas fight out of the way early, then start over fresh and see where you land.)

Faith. Often used by religious fundamentalists as the basis on which to discriminate, although this isn't purely a religious pre-serve. I like to see faith as the practice of maintaining, deep down, that things won't always be bad, that there will be good things to marvel at again and good people to surprise us by doing them. Maybe we'll even be the good guys. I honestly don't care what you believe in. I'm delighted, whatever gets you through the night, or the Christmas fight. If you go to Mass every week – even *every day* like those ladies in hats with net veils used to when I was a kid – that's great. If you meditate to a Buddha statue, fair play to you. You worship nature? I'm roasting – maybe we should listen to you more. Maybe, like me, you think it all ends at the end so we better make this bit count. There's room for all of us. But what we believe is almost never who we are: it's not a useful label for a person.

Ah, yes: generalising and labelling, singling out the worst traits exhibited by fundamentalists in any group, isn't smart: it can always be flipped and applied to a fundamentalist from within your own. Sexism, violence, a need to control: I've seen atheists exhibit all of these while condemning Islam. Some of the least charitable acts against me personally of late have been by self-proclaimed proud Christians. Some lads are excellent feminists and some women have internalised their own misogyny so deeply they don't even realise it's there. Tags are only broadly helpful. If it gives people solace in years like these, though, I'm envious of their conviction.

Regardless of personal beliefs (or lack thereof), I feel it can only be good to be excited at some things being unknowable, to there still being questions. What we know or are capable of knowing can change. I want to stay open, in case I miss something huge, like how there's a gravity switch at Earth's core and maybe WE WERE ABLE TO FLY ALL ALONG. Being wrong – even self-wrong-teous – and admitting it isn't a bad thing. Who am I to say yer wan isn't talking directly to angels? I don't believe she is, but even if I could scientifically prove it's due to what some would call a flaw in her wiring, if it's making her happy, why would I deprive her of that comfort?

I will never understand the need to impose beliefs (or lack thereof) on others. Live your life and if it looks like it's working, people might ask you about it. Dogma is a pain in the hole, whether it's how you worship or your new clean-eating regime. It's important not to replace faith with a kind of faithless zealotry. I get it; finding your way out of indoctrination and into a new set of beliefs is exhilarating; you so desperately want everyone else to experience the joy of giving up gluten that you go around slapping scones out of people's hands. But some people still like scones. You don't have to eat them. You do you, and let them and their scones do them. Which leads us back to peace.

Let's bin the idea that saying *we all deserve the same basic rights* is just another form of scone-slapping dogma. It isn't, though it's been fun to watch linguistic gymnasts limber up for this one during The Shitness. The best thing the far right have achieved in recent times is the potential for the inclusion of Linguistic Gymnastics in the actual Olympics. I look forward to watching them wrap their tongues around the parallel bars. Suggesting people not impose their beliefs on others is not asking anyone to discard those beliefs. You lose nothing by asking for equality. You're sharing love in a hopeless place and being more like Rihanna, even in a small way, is always a win.

I've seen many of my own beliefs shatter recently (Bowie and Carrie and George not being immortal, for instance). I'm clinging to one last belief like a life-raft: that people basically do want good for others. It's only fear that makes us cruel.

I've said it a lot, I know, but feel it's worth its place as a just-before-parting shot: I believe that kindness is stronger, braver and tougher than anything else right now. I am trying to be strong, brave and tough.

I hope we all can. I know we can. Or, at least, I have faith.

77

HANDS OFF OUR HANDS: IN DEFENCE OF MASTURBATION

I have a secret admirer. He's a very important person and, although we've never met, I hear on the grapevine he thinks about me a lot. An older man, he's got a beautiful gaff, a unique car and a sexy accent, which, while fairly earthly, are on many a potential partner's deal-or-no-deal list, so I suppose I should be flattered. He doesn't even mind that I'm married – in fact, he prefers it. He just wishes I had kids too. Did I mention that the gaff was in Rome? And that my admirer was the Pope?

Yeah, *the* Pope. You'd think that with all the hours spent travelling and hearing VIP confessions and Windex-ing the Pope-mobile he'd hardly have time to think about little old me day and night. But he does. And don't worry, he thinks about you too, and what you're doing with your filthy, filthy hands.

When I read that the Vatican had produced an exhortation (*Amoris Laetitia – The Joy of Love*) – a kind of fancy parish bulletin which was rumoured to include plenty of masturbation – I was intrigued, then disappointed, and then not one bit surprised to discover that it was, of course, against it. And now I was thinking about it – yes, thinking about masturbating, thanks Vatican! – and wondering, what does the Church have against hand-love? It's just a bit of solo rubbing, isn't it? Or maybe not so solo, and maybe not hands, but who cares?

They do, apparently. Deeply. Mmm, yeah.

Of course there were plenty of other things we were all being told not to do in this exhortation, and it's inspired almost as many think-pieces as Beyoncé's *Lemonade* (almost), but it's masturbation that's my favourite, so I'm going to play with that one. I want to grab this topic with all five fingers and tug at it a bit.

If it is your sincerely held religious belief that every sperm is sacred, that's fine; you go ahead and keep your seed in its tube – it's your tube, after all. You do you. (Sorry, I just remembered you're against that). But where do these auld lads in Italy get off exhorting the rest of us not to do it? Answer: they don't get off at all. Or that's what they would have us believe. If you ask me, there's a reason their robes are loose and flowing, and there's a very real possibility that those hands, folded in their laps in prayer, are fake. Some of those synods are very long, after all. You'd get bored. Those auld lads are human and we all have needs, and many of us are two-faced hypocrites as we all know.

If it's worry over seed-spill that has them so buzzed about our solo flights, then why aren't women allowed to do it? We don't have seed to spill and I've certainly never laid an egg during a personal sesh. We know why. It's because pleasure is forbidden unless we're planning on pregnancy, which we're supposed to do every time. Then we can have one demure pre-baby orgasm as a treat and that's it. Forever. Close 'em up, down below, you won't be needed for nine months! As for the clitoris, well, you won't be needing that again at all.

Why would you want to deprive anyone of one of the most fun, free things you can do? And you want to know, Vatican lads, why you weren't invited to my last birthday party.

- Masturbation is better than alcohol: it gets you high without harming your liver (if it does, there's a chance you may have gone too far).

- Masturbation has zero calories, therefore it's completely guilt-free, according to the rules of magazines and health-food ads.

- You can masturbate during a power cut: you don't need WiFi and there will be no bill, even if you have a heavy usage quarter.

- You don't need a significant other: your significant other is you. You may not be able to give yourself a cuddle, but you can have hours of fun perfecting your digital technique. AND YOU DON'T HAVE TO DO IT AT ALL, if sex isn't your thing. It's completely up to you; no one can force you. Hurrah!

I understand that a lot of what my secret boyfriend (the Pope, not my right hand) and his organisation do is based on maintaining power. For example, celibacy came about so Church funds didn't get passed on to family. But this rule just makes no sense at all. I don't see any reason why masturbation couldn't even be included in meditation, elevated to some kind of worship. Couldn't this be one of the things people offer up?

Some of you will have read this column and winced. *Disgusting!* But why? Why is it disgusting? Masturbation has saved relationships, it boosts mental health and physical well-being, relieves stress, alleviates loneliness, enhances naps and literally no one else is affected in any way. That's kind of a beautiful thing. We just don't talk about it enough. Oh, no, no, no: I don't want to know the ins and outs of your rubbing life. I just mean that if we don't talk about it in a healthy and positive way, the auld lads in Rome will keep on trying to make people ashamed of it.

Regardless of their exhortations and obsession with the rest of us, I assure you, they know a thing or two about the view of painted ceilings, if you know what I mean. Flat on their backs and all that. And they need to get a grip.

EPILOGUE

ADDING PETROL TO THE BONFIRE

This piece was originally my second-last weekly column for Head-Stuff. The penultimate one. I always get a bit wary when anything is called 'ultimate': roller coasters, fighters, burgers. It literally means 'the last', and I'd be happier with a slightly substandard roller coaster/fighter/burger if it meant I got to experience a few more.

I enjoyed the idea of calling the collection *Rage-In*: *raging*, and all that. Haha. My chance to vent in a (usually, hopefully) funny way that might entertain or offer some catharsis for others feeling the anger too. Sometimes, as you'll have seen, I was just self-wrong-teously angry. There's no escaping the fact that stuff's broken; the system's rotten and I have no solutions. Got nothing, like I've said. Platitudes won't cut it. They're insulting.

What I definitely don't want to do is contribute to the rage, to the white noise that's the backdrop of this point in history. Even in a funny way. And so, I stopped writing Rage-In for HeadStuff.

It was brilliant to have an outlet so cool and fun and socially conscious (despite the evil bosses and having to live at HeadStuff HQ). Let me tell you, it's a relief to no longer be trapped with the rest of the contributors, subsisting on bad coffee and better-than-average WiFi. They were good times, but now I am free.

How have I filled the weeks since? There was some initial de-compressing. Heavy counselling. It's possible I'm institutionalised and don't even realise it. Best to start with getting some air – breathe in, breathe out – and take it from there.

Instead of the gruelling rounds with a punchbag I needed to get me in form for Rage-In, maybe I'll try some super-still, super-chill yoga – statue yoga, if there's such a thing. If there isn't, maybe I'll invent it. I'd be happy to tour the world bringing people peace by telling them not to move. That's the kind of guru I plan to become once I manage to leave the rage behind.

Rage's only purpose is to turn it into action. Commentating, stoking from the sidelines and doing nothing, well, I call bullshit. Now, I want to write bullshit, maybe even beautiful bullshit: what I don't want to do is add to a mounting pile of fear and inertia.

Because I'm scared. I'm genuinely scared by what I see out there. It's overwhelming and that's when we freeze – which is only okay when doing statue yoga with an instructor who is well-trained (and well-paid: cash please, or cool yoga stuff). We can't afford to freeze. And so I don't really want to write about the world any more, not in that way. I'll leave that to journalists and the Muddeners who say they hate the journalists but really wish they were them.

Someone else may come and take up my HeadStuff slot, someone young and dynamic and much, much better at being topical AND funny. I will rage about that, silently, inwardly: I will do it in a way that won't infect you.

Or maybe my slot will remain empty, and internet wags will deem the blank space better than what I wrote every week. Maybe people will stop by and wonder again what was the name of the person who wrote a thing here? Tanya something? Maybe no one will come. Maybe I was never there at all.

Breathe in. Breathe out.

Yours, spent of rage,

Flynn.

ACKNOWLEDGEMENTS

They are evil, but I suppose I should thank Paddy O'Leary and Alan Bennett, the bosses at HeadStuff. They made me do it and are the reason why this book exists. HeadStuff is a beautiful thing, not really evil at all, and it was lovely to have the space to write what I felt each weird week, with support and fun from the office.

Big thanks to Noel O'Regan – a patient man with an unparalleled sense of structure – who helped take my weekly ramblings and turn them into a book. To all at Mercier Press: up Cork!

Thanks to Ruth Connolly for the cover shots and being nothing like the scary photographers in the 'Don't Shoot' piece.

Thanks to the Abbey Theatre and This Is Pop Baby, in particular Philly McMahon, for giving CPR to dreams I'd thought had flatlined.

To my agents (Mandy, Charlie, Deborah, Leigh), with me through thick, thin and cheap-ass producers.

To everyone involved in the Repeal campaign: you take a lot of shit and have been there for me when I've been on the receiving end. Thank you.

To my family, who've picked me up again and again: Mum and Sara and Carl. Grateful forever and always.

And to writer friends who keep gently pushing and nudging and comforting so we all keep going and do better: you rock. If we're truthful, kind, get it wrong, do better, keep going, maybe it'll be all right. Maybe. I hope.